郭清輝先生
譚敏惠女士惠存

彭文
二〇〇九年庚寅春

Zhao Bao
Tai Chi Kung Fu

Author Wayne Peng
Translator Yuhwa Liao Rozelle

趙堡太極拳

彭文 著

廖玉華 譯

美國太極文化協會 出版
Published by USA Tai Chi Culture Association

Zhao Bao Tai Chi Kung Fu

Published by **USA Tai Chi Culture Association**
Copyright©2008 USA Tai Chi Culture Association
All rights reserved. No part of this publication may be reproduced without the written permission of USA Tai Chi Culture Association。
所有編輯內容及圖片，都受美國著作權及國際條約的保護，由美國太極文化協會保留一切權利，未經過書面同意不得復制。

ISBN	978-0-615-25566-8
Author	Wayne Peng
Translator	Yuhua Liao
Editor	Sophia Bo Zhou
	Shuh-Hai Wong
Publisher	USA Tai Chi Culture Association
Address	1344 Ridder Park Drive, San Jose, CA 95131, USA
Mailing Address	P.O.Box 361551, Milpitas, CA 95036, USA
Telephone	1-408-262-3867 1-510-739-1832
Website	www.usataichikungfu.com
Email	tcca@usataichikungfu.com

太極之光

贈彭文先生

應武當山武當拳法研究會
武當雜誌社囑 丁亥夏 劉紀敏書

美國太極文化協會
USA TAI CHI CULTURE ASSOCIATION
www.usataichikungfu.com   tcca@usataichikungfu.com

趙堡太極

　　美國太極文化協會是由世界著名武術家、國際太極大師彭文先生倡導創立的非謀利公益國際武術專業組織，其宗旨是推廣傳播中國優秀的傳統武術文化，以中華傳統武術瑰寶太極拳爲橋梁促進東西方文化的交融，在世界範圍弘揚中國古典哲學之動靜相間、剛柔相濟，身心兼修等和諧理念。

　　美國太極文化協會會長彭文先生專業致力于在國際間傳播太極拳，同時任美國加州中醫藥大學太極氣功養生防身研究中心主任、碩士/博士生導師、美國太極學院院長、美國太極功夫俱樂部總教練、國際太極易拳道總會總教練、太極易拳道黑帶八段、國際武術散手道聯盟理事、武術散手道黑帶八段，中國武術刊物《武當》、《太極》多次刊登其專業論文并榮登雜志封面人物，并入編《中國體育年鑒》《世界著名武術家風采》《當代中華武壇精英名錄》，同時擔任海外編委及特邀研究員。

美國太極文化協會
1344 Ridder Park Dr., San Jose, CA95131, USA
郵政信箱：
P.O.Box 361551, Milpitas, CA95036, USA
電話：001-408-262-3867　001-510-386-9378
Email:tcca@usataichikungfu.com
Website:www.usataichikungfu.com

-3-

世界拳王Holyfield and Tai Chi Master Peng

Master Peng and His Students

Master Peng and TCCA Members

Master Peng and Gao, Zhan Sheng, China Consul General at 2008 Olympic Torch Relay Celebration Party

TCCA Members Join 2008 Olympic Torch Relay in San Francisco

KMVT Station Interview Master Peng for Zhao Bao Tai Chi Kung Fu

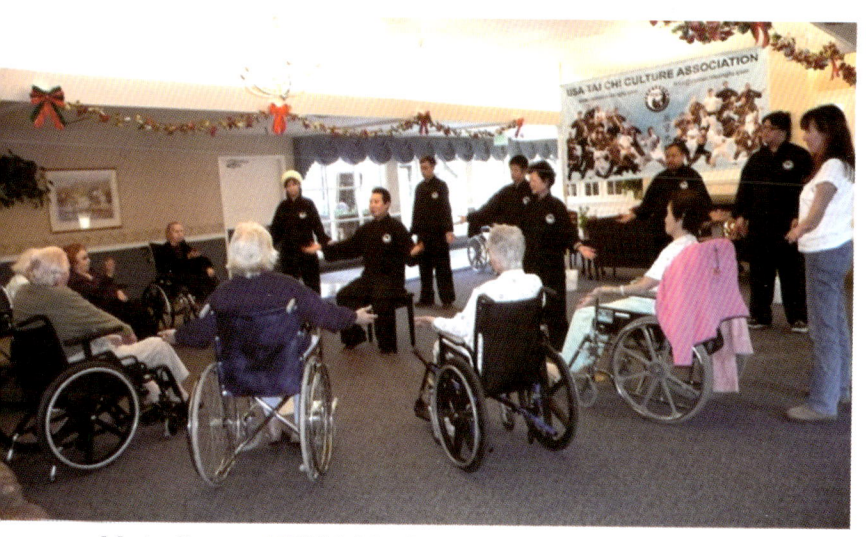

Master Peng and TCCA Members Join Charitable Activities

Master Peng and His Students Visit Wudang Mountains

USA & China Tai Chi Seminar

USA Tai Chi Culture Association

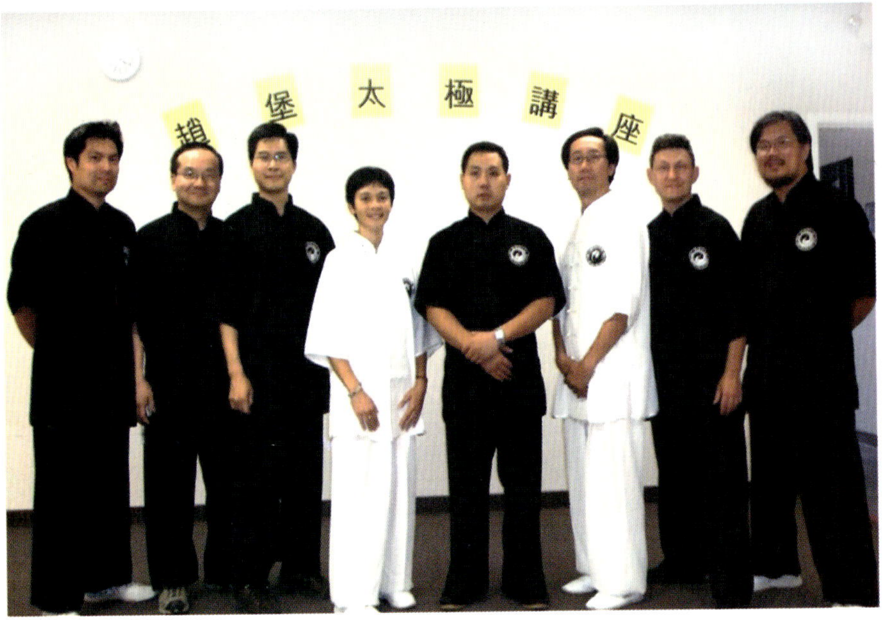
趙堡太極講座

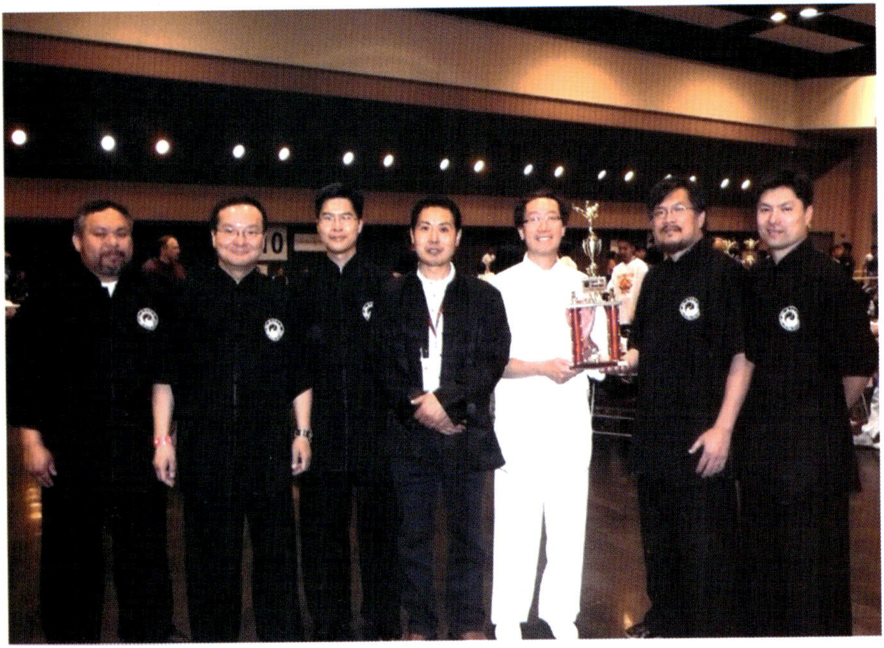

Henry Carrabello , Master Peng and Wei Jim Lai

彭文大師與其弟子陳志生和黃光南

天王托塔　　　　　　　　童子拜佛

關公脫袍	神龍擺尾
凌空發放	霸王裁椿
倒卷烏龍	閻羅脫靴

Zhao Bao Tai Chi Master of Age   趙堡太極拳歷代宗師

- 1st Jiang Fa — 蔣發 
- 2nd Xing Xi Huai — 邢希懷 
- 3rd Zhang Chu Chen — 張楚臣 
- 4th Chen Jing Bo — 陳敬伯 
- 5th Zhang Zong Yu — 張宗禹 
- 6th Zhang Yan — 張彥 
- 7th Chen Qing Ping — 陳清平 
- 8th He Zhao Yuan — 和兆元 
- 9th He Qing Xi — 和慶喜 
- 10th ZhengWu Qing — 鄭悟清 
- 11th Song Yun Hua — 宋蘊華 
- 12th Wayne Peng — 彭文

赵堡太极拳历代传人传承表
Lineage of Zhao Bao Tai Chi

| 太极拳创始人 | Legendary Founder |
| 張三丰祖师 | Zhang San-Feng |

↓

| 太极拳理论集大成者 | The Tai Chi Theorist |
| 王宗岳宗师 | Wang Zong-Yue |

↓

第一代	蒋 发	1st Generation	Jiang Fa
第二代	邢希怀	2nd Generation	Xing Xi-Huai
第三代	张楚臣	3rd Generation	Zhang ChuChen
第四代	陈敬伯	4th Generation	Chen Jing-Bo
第五代	张宗禹	5th Generation	Zhang Zong-Yu
第六代	张 彦	6th Generation	Zhang Yan
第七代	陈清平	7th Generation	Chen Qing-Ping
第八代	和兆元	8th Generation	He Zhao-Yuan
第九代	和庆喜	9th Generation	He Qing-Xi
第十代	郑悟清	10th Generation	Zheng Wu-Qing
第十一代	宋蕴华	11th Generation	Song Yun-Hua
第十二代	彭 文	12th Generation	Wayne Peng

太极

2006 3

竞赛套路与传统套路动作要领辨析
太极拳与方圆
传统太极拳57年之变迁

Preface (1)

Mr. Peng is cheerful, lively, and intellectual. I believe these should be the characteristics basic to the personality of a taichi practitioner. A Chinese proverb says: A sage cures illness before it occurs. What does it mean to cure illness before it occurs? It means prevention. Before possible illness occurs, a sage already starts to prevent it from happening. Taichi is like a sage. It does not wait until health problems occur to cure them. It is wonderful in this way. And the result of doing taichi correctly is to be like Mr. Peng, who is cheerful, lively and intellectual.

Taichi Kungfu, as people often speak of it, includes both body and technique. The bodily aspect suggests health, and the technique aspect suggests combat. Considering the history of taichi over the last one hundred years, I see that taichi was more concerned with fighting at first, then focused on both health and fighting, and now concentrates more on health. Of course, fighting techniques and health improvement cannot really be separated from each other. Although I am not completely sure, I believe that taichi is mainly practiced for the purpose of health improvement at the present time. Now Mr. Peng's taichi is full of the flavor of ancient times. It is both rich in health improvement, and clear in fighting techniques. It is rare and commendable.

People also say that after you have become skillful in whatever you are doing, you understand its philosophy. Through practicing taichi, you learn the philosophy of people and society. Mr. Peng is not old, but he is already going in this direction. How do I know? I know because of this book.

I wrote this preface to show my delight in the publication of this book, and to congratulate Mr. Peng.

Managing editor of the Chinese magazine *Tai Chi*
Yang Zongjie
July 2008

Preface

序一

　　彭文先生很陽光、朝氣，外加一份儒雅。在某種程度上，我覺得這是一位太極拳人應具備的形象和氣質。聯繫起中國有句古語叫"聖人治未病"。什么叫"未病"？就是"未發病"。尚未發病，就開始治療，這才叫聖人。那么與此相反，世俗之人就往往是等到健康出了問題才去治。凡聖之間，僅此而已。而太極拳，堪稱"聖人"，她是最善長"治未病"的。那么治未病的效果，就會表現出一種陽光、朝氣和儒雅的形象和氣質!

　　人們談到太極拳，常用到一個詞，"體用兼備"。體指完善自身，用指技藝對抗。據愚觀察百多年太極拳史，太極拳有一個從用到體用再到體的發展脈絡。當然用中有體，體中有用，愚在此只是舉其大略，欲分出各個不同時期的不同側重。比如現時就是太極拳以體為主的一個時代。此語雖不敢十分肯定，但感覺此一起伏綫依稀可辨。今觀彭文先生之太極拳，覺其古意濃濃，體之外，用很清，則體用兼顧，實屬難得。

　　人們又說太極拳乃"技而進乎道也"，就是說雖在習拳，卻可從中悟出人與社會的大道理。彭文先生雖很年輕，卻正在向這方面發展。何以見得，此書可見。

　　聊以上邊數語，以示愚對此書付梓的欣喜祝賀之情。

中國《太極》雜誌社 總編
楊宗杰
二零零八年七月

Preface (2)

Mr. Wayne Peng is a world-renowned grandmaster of Zhaobao Taichi Kungfu. I have known him for a few years. His technique is deep and wonderful in taichi, push-hands, and grappling. But not until last year at the 20th annual celebration of the International Wushu Sanshoudao Association did I finally have a chance to see his extraordinary performance.

Mr. Peng's movements were so graceful and smooth that they refreshed the eyes. Sometimes he moved like a gentle spring breeze on a willow tree, and sometimes he moved like frenzied wind and sudden rain. All of his movements were intrinsically connected. In Mr. Peng's technique the soft is inside the hard, and the hard is inside the soft. This characteristic is unique to Zhaobao Taichi, and in this way Zhaobao Taichi is very different from the other five styles of traditional taichi. In the past, some people have categorized Zhaobao Taichi as one of the branches of Chen-style Taichi. But after I watched Mr. Peng's performance, I realized that these two styles are completely different. The techniques of Zhaobao Taichi form a style totally of its own. By watching Mr. Peng's performance, I learned that Zhaobao Taichi is supreme among the styles of kungfu, and is replete with profound techniques. It is most valuable for health improvement and self-defense. The techniques of Zhaobao Taichi should be made available for people to observe and learn. I believe that Zhaobao Taichi kungfu is one of the treasures of Chinese martial arts.

The culture of taichi includes the traditional Chinese philosophies of *The Book of Changes* and *The Doctrine of the Mean*. It has aspects of yin-yang theory, martial arts, biology, human anatomy, health, cosmology, Daoism, Confucianism, Buddhism, Zen, spiritualism, psychology, medicine, military studies, and more. It is one of the essential cultures of the world. The publication of Mr. Peng's book *Zhaobao Taichi Kungfu* will help people all over the world to understand Zhaobao Taichi better. I think it is a great contribution to the study of Chinese martial arts. I congratulate Mr. Peng, and I hope Zhaobao Taichi will be brought to even greater heights.

Shouyu Liang
Chairman of International Wushu Sanshoudao Association

序 二

　　彭文先生是國際著名的趙堡太極拳大師，我認識他已經有好幾年了。他在太極推手、擒拿等方面根底很深，直到去年在國際武術散手道聯盟二十周年慶典的大型表演會上才看到他精彩的表演，他那瀟灑流暢的動作令人眼目一新，時而如春風吹拂楊柳，時而如狂風驟雨，連綿不斷，柔中有剛，剛中有柔，這種獨特的風格和其它五種傳統太極拳是不同的，過去有人把趙堡太極歸類于陳氏太極拳中的一支，但看了彭文先生的表演后，我覺得風格完全不同。趙堡太極拳完全是自成體系，觀察彭文先生的表演，可看出趙堡太極是非常精華的拳種，個中深藏玄機，其健身和技擊作用都是很高的，是很值得推廣弘揚的一種拳法，是我中華武庫的珍寶之一。

　　太極文化包羅了中華文化中的哲學、易學、陰陽學、武學、生物學、生命學、養生學、宇宙學、道學、儒學、佛學、禪學、玄學、中庸學、心理學、醫學、軍事學等等各個方面；也是世界文化的精髓部分。

　　彭文先生《趙堡太極拳》一書的出版，讓世界人民了解趙堡太極，是對弘揚中華武術的一大貢獻。特此向彭文先生祝賀，也祝願趙堡太極更加發揚光大。

國際武術散手道聯盟
主席 梁守渝
2008年7月13日

Foreword

Zhaobao Tai Chi is one of the oldest traditional schools of taichi in China. It has many hundreds of years of history. It is well-known in the world of martial arts. And it is the origin of the Wǔ 武, hǎo 郝, and Sūn 孫 schools of taichi.

Because of the constraints of feudal thinking, the kungfu, technique, and theoretical books of Zhaobao Taichi were passed on to only one person in each generation for seven generations up to modern times. Therefore, it was unknown to outsiders. People knew only that the secrets of Zhaobao Taichi were kept in its own village. For a long time, people did not have an opportunity to understand the characteristics of Zhaobao Taichi. Finally during the 1930's, in the 10th generation successor of Zhaobao Taichi kungfu masters, Master Zhèng Wùqīng and Master Zhèng Bóyīng separately left the town of Zhaobao and ended the long history of Zhaobao Taichi remaining isolated in its own village. Master Zhèng Wùqīng and Master Zhèng Bóyīng both settled in Xi'an. They put down roots in the northwest part of China and spent the remainder of their lives teaching Zhaobao Taichi kungfu. In the 11th generation successor of Zhaobao Taichi masters, Master Sòng Yùnhuá went abroad during the 1980's. He was the first person to bring Zhaobao Taichi kungfu to Hong Kong, Macau, Thailand, Singapore, Japan, France, Germany, and Holland. People outside of China finally had the opportunity to learn about Zhaobao Taichi kungfu.

Zhaobao Taichi kungfu is one of the best types of exercise for health improvement and self-defense. Its fighting techniques are profound. It is one of the treasures of Chinese tradition and culture. It is well-known in the world not only because its movements are full of rhythm and beauty, and look natural

Foreword

and elegant, but also because those movements are powerful and effective in fighting. Zhaobao Taichi is valuable and useful for strengthening one's body, concentrating one's mind, cultivating one's personality, warding off illness, and enriching one's spiritual life. Zhaobao Taichi is good for everybody to learn and practice, regardless of one's age, gender, and health. There is no need for a large space to practice, and there is no need for expensive machines. According to what people say in Zhaobao Village, all it takes is the space for a cow to lie down. You may practice it indoors or outdoors, as you wish. People should do it according to their health. Now taichi exercises have become popular throughout the world and many people love them. In the modern materialistic world, people have come to realize the importance of strengthening their bodies. Many people are enthusiastic about the practical use of Zhaobao Taichi kungfu.

In this book I introduce the traditional theory of Zhaobao Taichi kungfu and provide exercises. I include pictures of the positions, and I analyze the techniques of push-hands, grappling, and san shou of Zhaobao Taichi kungfu. I hope it will help you to understand. If this book can be an inspiration or pleasure for anyone who loves martial arts, it will bring happiness to me as the writer.

Wayne Peng
July, 2008, in San Francisco

前言

　　趙堡太極拳是中國最古老傳統的太極拳流派之一，距今已有數百年的歷史，在武術界享有極高的聲譽，當前流傳于世的武式、郝式、孫式等太極拳流派，皆淵源於趙堡太極拳。

　　由于受中國舊時代封建宗法觀念的束縛，趙堡太極傳統拳技、功法以及理論書籍曾一直在少數拳師中秘本單傳七代之久，其間極少外流，自古就有"趙堡太極不出村"之說；致使在較長的一段歷史時期，人們無法全面了解趙堡太極拳之風貌。直到二十世紀三十年代，趙堡太極拳第十代宗師鄭悟清先生和鄭伯英先生，先後走出趙堡古鎮，才徹底結束了"趙堡太極不出村"的歷史。二公相繼定居西安，立足西北，面向全國，廣泛傳授趙堡太極拳藝，以畢生心血弘揚光大。後趙堡太極拳第十一代宗師宋蘊華先生又在二十世紀八十年代末走出國門，率先將趙堡太極拳推廣到港、澳、泰國、新加坡、日本、法國、德國、荷蘭等歐亞地區；趙堡太極終于徹底揭開其神秘面紗，廣泛為世界人民所了解。

　　趙堡太極拳是一項極其有益于身心健康和技擊性很強的體育運動，也是中華民族傳統文化瑰寶之一。其以達觀優雅的自然節奏鍛煉方式和神奇莫測的搏擊技能稱著于世；趙堡太極拳對強壯體質，磨練意志，陶冶性情，祛病御敵以及豐富人們的精神生活都具有重要的價值和作用。學練趙堡太極拳人人皆宜，不受年齡性別和身體素質的限制，更不需要寬闊的運動場地和繁瑣昂貴的健身器械，只需有幾平方米的室內或室外空間（趙堡自古有拳打臥牛之地一說），男女老少均可根

Foreword

據自身的條件進行學習和鍛煉；隨着太極運動的廣泛普及，以及東西方文化的不斷交融，中華民族的這一古老文化以其不可取代的運動優點，已經深深的受到了世界各地人民大眾的珍愛，日趨發達的物質文明使人們認識到體育強身的重要性，有識之士同時對趙堡太極拳在防身自衛獨特功能的實用價值上，給予了高度的肯定和認可。

本書將系列介紹趙堡太極拳傳統技法理論，以及套路姿勢示範，并對推手、擒拿及散手技擊分解，簡明論述，圖文并茂，一目了然。

如果廣大的太極武術愛好者以及武林同道能從本書中得到啟發或玩味受益，筆者將感到不勝欣慰之至。

彭文
2008 年 7 月于舊金山

Contents

Preface	1
Foreword	5
Chapter 1 A Brief History of Tai Chi	13
Chapter 2 Zhao Bao Tai Chi Origin	17
Chapter 3 Tai Chi Master Wayne Peng	21
Chapter 4 Traditional Zhao Bao Taichi Theory	25
1. Tai Chi Theory	25
2. Ten Zhao Bao Tai Chi Theory	28
- First Essential Theory	28
- Second Essential Theory	31
- Third Essential Theory	33
- Fourth Essential Theory	35
- Fifth Essential Theory	37
- Sixth Essential Theory	40
- Seventh Essential Theory	42
- Eighth Essential Theory	44
- Ninth Essential Theory	47
- Tenth Essential Theory	50
3. The Five Skill Levels of Zhaobao Taichi Kungfu	54
4. The Five Primary Elements and the Eight Body Maneuvers of Zhaobao Taichi	61
5. The Fighting Techniques of Zhaobao Taichi Kungfu	68

Contents

      6. Methods of Practicing Zhaobao Taichi Kungfu .. 75
      7. Tai Chi and Health 77

Chapter 5 Zhao Bao Tai Chi Routine 81
      1. The Seventy-Five Forms of Zhaobao
         Taichi Kungfu 81
      2. Illustrations of The Seventy-Five Movements
         of Zhaobao Taichi Kungfu........................ 88

Chapter 6 Zhao Bao Tai Chi Kung Fu 238
      1. Zhao Bao Tai Chi Push Hands 239
      2. Zhao Bao Tai Chi Qi Na (Grappling) 249
      3. Zhao Bao Tai Chi San Shou 262

Afterword 275

To Readers 278

目錄

序	…………………………………………	2
前言	…………………………………………	7
第一章	太極拳概論 ……………………………	16
第二章	趙堡太極拳源流 ………………………	20
第三章	趙堡太極拳大師彭文簡介 ……………	23
第四章	趙堡太極拳傳統理論 …………………	27

   1. 太極拳論 ……………………………………… 27
   2. 趙堡太極傳統總論十章 ……………… 30
     ● 一要論 ………………………………… 30
     ● 二要論 ………………………………… 32
     ● 三要論 ………………………………… 34
     ● 四要論 ………………………………… 36
     ● 五要論 ………………………………… 39
     ● 六要論 ………………………………… 41
     ● 七要論 ………………………………… 43
     ● 八要論 ………………………………… 46
     ● 九要論 ………………………………… 49
     ● 十續論 ………………………………… 53
   3. 趙堡太極功夫五界論 ………………… 59
   4. 趙堡太極五行八法論 ………………… 65
   5. 趙堡太極拳技擊特點 ………………… 72
   6. 趙堡太極拳練法說明 ………………… 76
   7. 太極拳與養生健身 …………………… 79

Contents

第五章　趙堡太極拳傳統套路 81
    1. 趙堡太極拳傳統七十五式套路名稱順序表 ... 81
    2. 趙堡太極拳傳統七十五式套路分解圖 88
第六章　趙堡太極拳技擊功夫 238
    1. 趙堡太極推手跌法 239
    2. 趙堡太極擒拿技法 249
    3. 趙堡太極散手搏擊 262
編后語 276
致讀者 279

Chapter 1
A Brief History of Tai Chi

In the central years of the Ming Dynasty (1400 A.D.) there lived a Daoist priest of the Wudang（武當） monastery named Zhang San Feng（張三豐）. According to legend, this revered ascetic often ventured deep into the wilds of the mountains to gather apothecary herbs. During one of his journeys, he chanced upon a fight between a white crane and a snake, and the combat of the two beasts struck him with inspiration. Combining concepts from the *Book of Changes* (*I Ching*) with the *Doctrine of the Mean* and Neo-Confucian thought, Zhang San Feng（張三豐） united these philosophies with the traditional forms of Chinese martial skill to create a new style of martial art, a style that could be practiced by all ages, which would strengthen the body and teach self-defense. After his epiphany, Zhang San Feng（張三豐） left the monastery and gave his new martial art the name of "Tai Chi Chuan"—a name that continues to be used by generations today.

Later, Tai Chi Chuan was passed on to the Shanxi（山西） native Wang Zong Yue（王宗岳） who perfected the theory of Tai Chi in the *Treatise on Tai Chi Chuan*. This volume, which he penned for posterity, has since become known as the Tai Chi Chuan "bible."

Wang Zong Yue（王宗岳） was also responsible for spreading the art of Tai Chi Chuan into the plains of central China when he taught his skills to Master Jiang Fa（蔣發）of the town of Zhao Bao（趙堡） in the Henan（河南） province.

Chapter 1 A Brief History of Tai Chi

The quintessential objective of Tai Chi is to become as "hard as iron, soft as cotton, slippery as a fish, and tenacious as glue" and its stances express these ideals with an understated elegance that makes it one of the most beautiful martial arts in the world. Tai Chi movements are natural and unforced, and seek to emulate the grace of passing clouds and flowing water: drifting apart and then gathering together again with quiet finesse. But its philosophy of attack and defense draws inspiration from the sudden and deceptive nature of ocean waves—emphasizing change and malleability—to attack at the most unexpected moment to leave an opponent senseless.

Over time, the original style of Tai Chi has since evolved and branched into six major schools: Zhao Bao style（趙堡）, Chen style（陳式）, Yang style（楊式）, Wu style（武式）, another Wu Style（吳式） and Sun style（孫式）. Although all originated from the same source, each has developed its own unique fighting flair as Tai Chi Chuan practitioners have spread all around the globe.

---

1 In some versions of the legend, Zhang San Feng witnesses a crane trying to eat a snake, but is unable to lift the snake into the air because of the snake's "soft" resistance, meaning that the snake gave way at every point the crane attacked so that it could not get a solid grasp on the snake. In other stories, it's the crane's pliant nature that allows it to capture the snake and thus conquer it. The reactions of the animals inspired Zhang San Feng to create a "pliant" and "soft" martial art that could redirect an opponent's aggression in the defender's favor.

2 The name could also be translated as "The Absolute Fist." The word "chi," which means the source of all things, can be read as both an expression of the source of all energy as well as the achievement of an understanding of the universe—both of which are elements very important to the philosophy of the style.

Chapter 1 A Brief History of Tai Chi

3 This saying should actually be translated as, "tenacious as a fish bladder," stemming from a practice in ancient China to boil the air bladders of fish to make a sticky paste used for glue.

第一章
太極拳概論

　　大約在公元十四世紀,元末明初時,相傳武當道士張三豐真人因深入荒無人烟的深山絕壁采集草藥,偶然發現一白鶴與蛇相爭斗,頓受啟發,并以"易經"、"中庸"、"理學"為其理論骨架結合中華武術的傳統功夫而創拳術,用以養生延年及防身自衛,因張三豐出自道門,遂冠以"太極拳"之雅稱,后世沿用。

　　后經傳承人山西王宗岳宗師將太極理論更加完善化,著《太極拳論》以傳后世,被奉為太極拳界的"聖經"。王宗岳傳河南趙堡鎮人蔣發(世人稱蔣把式-太極神手);方使此太極神功風靡中原大地。

　　太極拳素以"硬如鋼、軟如棉、滑如魚、粘如鰾"稱著于天下,其功架姿勢雅靜優美、和諧自然,運動如同行雲流水,飄然逸群,其技擊變化雲譎波詭,驚世駭俗,令人撲朔迷離,饒有哲理之豐采。

張三豐祖師

　　太極拳在其發展傳播的歷史長河里,開枝散葉,逐漸形成為:趙堡、陳式、楊式、武式、吳式、孫式等六大門派,其同出一源,各有特色,爭奇斗艷,目前太極拳習練者已遍及世界各地。

Chapter 2
Zhao Bao Tai Chi Origins

The Zhao Bao style of Tai Chi (赵堡太极拳) originated from the town of Zhao Bao (赵堡镇) in the sixteenth century. Located fourteen kilometers east of the county of Wen (温县) in the central Chinese province of Henan (河南), Zhao Bao is known for its idyllic atmosphere. The town looks south over the Yellow River's northern banks, and gazes north into the Taihang foothills, turning east into the capital (京畿), and extending west toward Luo Yi (絡伊). Since antiquity, this propitious location has made Zhao Bao a center of travel and trade. According to legend, Zhao Bao was once the elaborate Jin Yin Zhong burial grounds of the soldiers of Zhao Dynasty during the Warring States Period (500 B.C.–221 B.C.); thus earning the town the title of "Zhao Bao" or "Zhao's stronghold," a name which has continued into usage today.

In the closing years of the Ming Dynasty (1368–1644), the town's name became well-known in the world of martial arts when a Zhao Bao native named Jiang Fa (蒋发) studied Tai Chi under Shan Xi (山西) master Wang Zong Yue. Jiang Fa later chose fellow townsmen Xing Xihuai (邢希怀) as a worthy disciple to on pass his own skills to, and thus began an illustrious new tradition of martial arts in Zhao Bao Zhen. During the Kanxi Dynasty (1654 A.D.--1722 A.D.), the later emperor Yong Zheng (雍正) visited Zhao Bao and admired the Tai Chi grandmasters so much that he gifted a handwritten inscription to the local Temple of Guandi (关帝庙) to commend the martial prowess of the Zhao Bao Tai Chi masters.

17

Chapter 2 Zhao Bao Tai Chi Origins

The tenets of Zhao Bao Tai Chi emphasize simplicity, stressing that one should be as "hard as iron, soft as cotton, slippery as a fish, and tenacious as glue." Its philosophy is expressed in the composition of its stances, in movements that harmonize and flow with the anatomy of the human body. Its aesthetic draws inspiration from nature with the goal of achieving movement as light as a cloud and as fluid as water. The martial art derives the structure of its theory from canonical Chinese scriptures including, "I Ching"(易經) (The Book of Change), "Zhongyong"(中庸) (The Doctrine of the Mean), as well as Neo-Confucian thought ("理学"), uniting "The Three Teachings" (Confucianism, Buddhism, and Daoism), under a new umbrella of thought. Its art of attack and defense emulates the inscrutable shifts of clouds as well as the deceptively smooth pull of powerful ocean waves, attacking at the most unexpected to leave an opponent senseless.

Zhao Ba Tai Chi is still evolving in the long river of history. For seven generations Zhao Bao's conservative leaders kept the art exclusively within the clan, giving rise to the saying that, "Zhao Bao Tai Chi would never leave its village." Towards the end of the nineteenth century, however, this direct line of descent was broken, and many new practitioners entered the school. Then, in the 1930s, tenth generation Zhao Bao Tai Chi Grandmasters Zheng Wuqing (郑悟清, 1895–1984) and Zheng Boying (郑伯英, 1906–1961) both left Zhao Bao, respectively, and brought a definitive end to the axiom that "Zhao Ba Tai Chi would never leave its village." The two Grandmasters both settled in the nearby city of Xi'an and dedicated their lives to cultivating and promoting the art of Tai Chi to the greater public.

Chapter 2 Zhao Bao Tai Chi Origins

In the 1990s, Zhao Bao Tai Chi's eleventh generation Grandmaster Song Yun-Hua （宋蘊華）and Master Wayne Peng(彭文), the twelfth generation successor of Zhao Bao Tai Chi, took the reach of Zhao Bao Tai Chi even further — to Hong Kong as well as overseas — and their work has received worldwide acclaim.

The original inscription, "乾坤正气," is almost untranslatable into English. The first half of the phrase, "qian kun," refers to the balance of the sky and earth, and man's place between them in Daoist philosophy. Maintaining this balance is often the root of great strength. The second half, "zheng chi," can literally be translated as "straight air" but may be more accurately translated as referring to an aura of righteousness. Put together, "Qian Kun Zheng Chi" was high praise for the great depth of understanding and harmony that the Zhao Bao practitioners had achieved.

This saying is actually translated as, "tenacious as a fish bladder," stemming from a practice in ancient China to boil the air bladders of fish to make a sticky paste used for glue.

19

第二章
趙堡太極拳源流

趙堡太極拳發祥地趙堡鎮，位於中國河南溫縣東十四華里處，是一個典型的中國北方集鎮。趙堡鎮南眺黃河北堤，北望太行山麓，東達京津，西接洛伊；自古以來交通便利，商業興隆。傳說戰國時期趙國曾屯兵於此地的金銀冢，故得名"趙堡"，后世沿用。

遠在明末清初，趙堡人蔣發師承山西王宗岳太極拳藝，后擇賢授藝于本鎮門人邢希懷，方使趙堡古鎮再以武術聞名遐邇。康熙年間，四皇子胤禎（雍正帝）慕名到趙堡鎮訪查太極高手，在趙堡鎮關帝廟親筆題字："乾坤正氣"借以褒揚趙堡太極拳師的高超武功。

趙堡太極拳素以"硬如剛，軟如棉，滑如魚，粘如鰾"稱著于天下，其功架姿勢雅靜優美，和諧自然，運動如行雲流水，飄然逸群。拳藝理論以"易經"，"中庸"，"理學"為其骨架，交融"三教"，奇思冥想，饒有哲理之豐采。其技擊變化雲譎波詭，驚世駭俗，令人撲朔迷離。

趙堡太極拳在其發展的歷史長河里。曾因保守的宗法觀念單傳七代，素有"趙堡拳不出村"之說。十九世紀末期，始破單傳門規，授徒多人。二十世紀三十年代，趙堡太極拳第十代宗師鄭悟清先生（1895—1984）和鄭伯英先生（1906-1961）先後走出趙堡古鎮，才徹底結束了"趙堡拳不出鎮"的歷史。二公相繼定居西安，以畢生心血弘揚光大太極拳藝，使其得以廣泛流傳。

趙堡太極拳第十一代宗師宋蘊華先生及其弟子趙堡太極拳第十二代傳人彭文先生于二十世紀八、九十年代，又將趙堡太極拳藝傳播于港、澳及世界各地，受到社會各界廣泛好評。

Chapter 3
Tai Chi Master Wayne Peng

Master Peng is the twelfth generation successor of the Zhaobao Tai Chi lineage. Due to his love of Chinese traditional culture and kung fu, Master Peng studied under the Master Yun-hua Song, the eleventh generation of the Chinese Wu Dang Zhao Bao Tai Chi lineage. For more than thirty years since childhood, Master Peng has perfected his art with hard work and dedication. His movements are smooth and graceful that can only be attained through a deep understanding of the essence of Zhao Bao Tai Chi. Tai Chi movements are based on the principals of "center, balance, and curvature," and are focused on "relaxation, serenity, and fluidity." Master Peng's movements can be slow or quick, and explicit or subtle. Master Peng demonstrates his mastery through push-hands, free-style fighting, throws, and various kinds of lock movements.

In addition, Master Peng is proficient in Tai Chi Qi Gong and accomplished in the fields of the Taoist and Confucius philosophies. He has a profound understanding of the meaning and practical usage of Wu Xing and Ba Gua in Tai Chi principles.

In recent years, Master Peng has dedicated himself to the spread of knowledge and education in Tai Chi. His scientific teaching method is based on the "4-step movement dissection" and "3 point body positioning." Such methods have shown excellent results among students. Master Peng has been repeatedly featured on the covers of and his writing has been presented in professional Chinese Kung Fu Magazines such as "Wu Dang", a nd "Tai Chi." Master Peng is also

Chapter 3 Tai Chi Master Wayne Peng

listed in the "Who's Who of Contemporary Chinese Kung Fu Masters"; "The Charisma of World-famous Martial Arts Virtuoso" and "China Sports Yearbook". As well, he has been presented the award of "Contemporary Chinese Kung Fu Master Award" to commemorate his contribution to the Tai Chi Kung Fu field and he wins gold medal of "The Charisma of World-famous Martial Arts Virtuoso". In addition, Master Peng has been invited by "Chinese International Wushu Cultural Development and Research Center" and "Contemporary Chinese Wushu Encyclopedia Editorial Committee" respectively to be the Member of Overseas Research Committee and the Principal Technical Consultant.

Currently, Master Peng is the Chairman of USA Tai Chi Culture Association; Director/professor of Five Branches University Tai Chi Qi Gong & Self-Defense Research Center; Head Coach of USA Tai Chi Kung Fu Club; Principal of USA Tai Chi Kungfu Academy; Head Coach of International I Quan Dao Association and the Consultant of International Wushu Sanshou Dao Association. His students are located everywhere in the world and are in every profession such as professors, military personnels, police officers, students, doctors, businessmen, lawyers, dancers, actors, and especially computer engineers are the most. The results of his teaching are what attracted such diverse group of people to study under him.

第三章

太極大師 --- 彭文

　　彭文大師是中國武當趙堡太極拳第十二代正宗傳人。由于其酷愛中國傳統文化和武術，自幼拜師于中國武當趙堡太極拳第十一代宗師宋蘊華教授門下，學習太極拳功夫；三十余年藝耕不輟、苦心追求，通達武當趙堡太極拳精髓；其拳姿雅靜、飄逸如鶴，似行雲流水，連綿不斷；行拳以中、正、平、圓為基根，以松、靜、順為主導；五行八法貫穿其中，運動速度可慢可快、動作姿勢可大可小，太極功夫技藝純熟，內力上乘；尤其精通太極推手、散手、跌法、擒拿格鬥及分筋錯骨采手技術，承恩師言傳身教，獨得功法要領，深悟其中三昧。

　　彭文大師同時精研太極氣功養生及博學中國傳統文化儒、釋、道哲理思想之精華，深知五行、八卦之奧妙所在及實際應用。

　　近年來，彭文大師專心致力于在國際間傳播太極拳，以科學的教學訓練模式："四步分解法"及"三點定位論"來教授學生，效果奇佳；中國專業武術刊物：《武當》、《太極》雜誌多次刊登其專業論文并榮登雜誌封面人物；鑒于彭文先生在武術太極領域的卓越經歷與杰出成就，特入編《中國體育年鑒》、《世界著名武術家風采》、《當代中華武壇精英名錄》并授予"當代中華武壇精英獎"及"世界著名武術家金獎"，同時《中國國際武術文化發展研究中心》及《當代中華武術大典編輯工作委員會》特聘彭文先生擔任海外編委及特邀研究員。

23

Chapter 3 Tai Chi Master Wayne Peng

彭文大師現任美國太極文化協會會長、美國加州中醫藥大學太極氣功養生防身研究中心主任、碩士/博士生導師、美國太極功夫俱樂部總教練、美國太極學院院長、國際太極易拳道總會總教練、國際武術散手道聯盟理事兼加州分會主席，其親授弟子已遍及世界各地、分布于各行各業，其中包括：在校學生、教師、軍人、警衛、警察、醫生、商人、律師、舞蹈藝人等各界人士，尤其以電腦工程師為多，良好的教學效果受到社會各界廣泛好評。

Chapter 4
Traditional Zhao Bao Taichi Theory

1. Tai Chi Theory

Taichi, the supreme ultimate, comes from wuchi, the absence of the ultimate. Taichi is the changing of motion and stillness, and the origin of yin and yang. Once a body moves, yin and yang are separated, and when it stops moving, yin and yang come back together into one. Nothing more, and nothing less. If it extends out, it will curve back in. In push-hands exercise or in combat, if the movement of your opponent's energy is hard, yours should be soft. This is the strategy of "following." Another strategy is letting your energy be glued to your opponent's in whatever direction your opponent's energy is moving. If your opponent's is moving fast, yours moves fast, and if your opponent's is moving slowly, yours moves slowly. Movements may change, but the principle remains the same. Once you are familiar with the movements, and understand how energy moves in one's body, you have reached the point of understanding taichi. This process takes a lot of hard work and a long time to master.

Clearing your mind of all thought, keeping your head up, and sinking your energy into your dantian is very important in taichi. Keep your body straight, and do not tilt it, The energy may suddenly disappear, or suddenly appear. If your opponent puts pressure on your left arm, you should conceal your energy on your left arm; if your opponent puts pressure on your right arm, you should conceal your energy on your right arm. You may make your movement high or low; you may take a big step forward or a quick step back. Every movement you do should be just right, without force. If you were to add the

Chapter 4 Traditional Zhao Bao Tai Chi Theory

weight of a feather or a fly, it would be too much. You must be so skillful that your opponent has no way of knowing what you are doing, but you must know exactly what your opponent is doing. There are many schools of combat in the world. Although styles may differ, in most of them the strong win over the weak and the slow lose to the fast. This is nature, and not a matter of learning. But with the skill of taichi, you can use four ounces of strength to throw an opponent who attacks you with one thousand pounds of force. A skillful taichi practitioner in his or her 80th or 90th year can still do it. Speed is not the key to winning.

Your body should move like the sliding weight of a steelyard, and rotate like a wheel of a cart. If you shift your body to one side or lower your body, your center of gravity should follow appropriately. Avoid keeping your body weight equally on both feet. You often see people who have practiced kungfu for many years but do not understand shifting their weight, so they end up defeated. It is because they do not realize their mistake of keeping their weight on both feet. In order to avoid the problem of rigidity, you have to understand that yin and yang are constantly in flux as they adjust to each other. Just as yin and yang can not be separated in their movements, you should harmonize your motion to the motion of your opponent, following as closely as if you were glued to him or her. When you understand that yin and yang are always moving together, then you understand how energy works. After you understand how energy works, the more you practice, the more skillful you get. Practice and learn until you can move your energy any way you want.

The key is to follow your opponent without asserting anything of your own. That is all. There is a Chinese proverb: A tiny error in the beginning will result in a huge mistake in the end. A slight error in this matter will result in defeat. It is not necessary to chase after complicated theories. The taichi learner must understand consequences. That is the purpose of this writing.

第四章
趙堡太極拳傳統理論

1. 太極拳論 -王宗岳

太極者，無極而生；動靜之機，陰陽之母也。動之則分，靜之則合。無過不及，隨曲就伸。人剛我柔謂之走，我順人背謂之粘。動急則急應，動緩則緩隨。雖變化萬端，而理惟一貫。由招熟而漸悟懂勁，由懂勁而階及神明。然非用功之久，不能豁然貫通焉。

虛靈頂勁，氣沉丹田。不偏不倚，忽隱忽現。左重則左虛，右重則右杳。仰之則彌高，俯之則彌深。進之則愈長，退之則愈促。一羽不能加，蠅蟲不能落。人不知我，我獨知人，英雄所向無敵，蓋皆由此而及也。

斯技旁門甚多，雖勢有區別，概不外壯欺弱、慢讓快耳。有力打無力，手慢讓手快，是皆先天自然之能，非關學力而有為也。察四兩撥千斤之句，顯非力勝，觀耄耋能御眾之形，快何能為！

立如秤準，活似車輪。偏沉則隨，雙重則滯。每見數年純功不能運化者，率皆自為人制，雙重之病未悟耳。欲避此病，須知陰陽。粘即是走，走既是粘。陰不離陽，陽不離陰，陰陽相濟，方為懂勁。懂勁后，愈練愈精，默識揣摩，漸至從心所欲。

本是舍己從人，多誤舍近求遠，所謂差之毫厘，謬之千里，學者不可不詳辯焉。是為論。

Chapter 4 Traditional Zhao Bao Tai Chi Theory

2. Ten Zhao Bao Tai Chi Theory

First Essential Theory   Unity

After things have been dispersed, they will be united in one, and after division, there will be unification. This is nature. Each thing between heaven and earth has its own place. Even though things look chaotic, all of them have a single origin, as they all belong to one original place. Taichi is no different. There are many theories about taichi. If your taichi is profound, you are, of necessity, capable of ten thousand changes. However you move, the posture of your movements is always correct, and your energy is always right. Although movements may be varied, there is only one energy behind them. The unity within a body connects everything together from the head to the feet, including internal organs, tendons, bones, muscles, skin, face, arms, and legs, forming the complete body. The body binds all parts together into one, and they cannot be separated. When your upper body desires to move, the lower body follows; when the lower body desires to move, the upper body leads; when the head and the legs move, the torso follows; and when the torso moves, the head and legs harmonize. The inside and outside are connected to each other, and the front and back respond to each other. This is what is called the unity of all parts.

So we know that in taichi, you do not make any movement by force, but rather by nature. When you are still, then be still like a mountain. When you strike, then strike like thunder rumbling or a mountain collapsing. Move as fast as lightning. When are still, your whole body is relaxed and your mind is not thinking about anything. When you move, your whole body moves together. All parts of your body move in one direction. It is like water descending, and nothing can stop the way it goes. Before you strike, it is as if all your energy is still inside a bomb, and when the bomb explodes, it is too late for people to cover their ears. There is no time for them to think, and it is no use for them to make decisions. As soon as it happens, it is already done.

If that is the way it is, you may ask, then what is the use of talking about it? Well, energy can be accumulated in time, and you can benefit from it. It takes a long time to practice taichi and achieve maturity in it. Study the taichi theories. Ask questions and fortify your knowledge. Sooner or later, things will become clear to you. In all things, seek knowledge. Knowledge is neither easy nor difficult, but everything depends on your hard work. Do not skip steps, and do not rush. Do first things first, progress step by step, and one day your body will be unified in one. Your whole body will be able to move together as one from head to foot, and from inside to outside. This is what is meant by saying: After things have been dispersed, they will be united in one, and after division, there will be unification. The body binds all parts together into one, and there is only one energy behind them.

2. 趙堡太極傳統總論十章 - 蔣發

一要論 （一體）

從來散之必有其統也，分之必有其合也，故天地間四面八方，紛紛者各有所屬；千頭萬緒，攘攘者自有其源。蓋一本而散為萬殊，而萬殊咸歸于一本；夫拳術之學亦不逾此理矣。

且拳事之論亦甚繁矣，斯技精而要之千變萬化，無往非勢，即無往非氣，勢雖不類，而氣歸于一。夫所謂一者，自頂至足，內而有臟腑筋骨，外而有肌肉皮膚、五官、四肢百骸，相聯為一貫者也。破之而不開，撞之而不散。上欲動而下自隨之，下欲動而上自領之，上下動而中部應之，中部動而上下和之。內外相連，前後相應，所謂以一貫之者，其斯之謂歟？

斯技毋須強橫取襲而為之也，而要非勉強以致之襲而為之也；當時而靜，寂然湛然，居其所而穩如山岳；當時而動，如雷如崩，出其手而疾如閃電。且靜無不靜，表裡上下全無參差牽挂之意；動無不動，前後左右并無抽扯游移之形。洵乎若水之就下，沛然而莫能御之也。若火機之內攻，發之而不及掩耳。不暇思索，不煩擬議，誠不期然而已然，莫之致而至。然豈無所至而雲乎？蓋氣以積月而有益，功以久練而方成。觀聖門一貫之傳，必俟多聞強識之后，抵豁然之境，不廢格物致知之功。是知事無難易，功惟自盡，不可躐等，不可急遽，按部就序，循次而進，夫而后百骸肢節自有貫通，上下表裡不難聯絡，庶乎散者統之，分者合之，四體百骸終歸于一氣矣。

Chapter 4 Traditional Zhao Bao Tai Chi Theory

Second Essential Theory   Yin and Yang

There are stars, energy, and many other kinds of things in the universe. Stars are born and die. They move in circles, not straight lines. Everything contrasts with everything else, but everything is also related to everything else. This is nature. Taichi is no different.

People who talk about taichi also talk about qi 氣, the energy in your body. There is only one qi. In general, we can call it the energy of breathing. However, for purposes of discussion, we can divide it into inhaling and exhaling. Inhaling is yin, and exhaling is yang. Taichi movements are closely related to breathing. There are breathing techniques in taichi. They are generally based on the theory of yin and yang.

Some ways to distinguish yin and yang are:
 Inhaling is yin, and exhaling is yang.
 Stillness is yin, and motion is yang.
 Downward movement, like the receding of a wave of yin-energy or yang-energy, is yin. Upward movement, like the thrust of a wave of yin-energy or yang-energy, is yang.

Another way to distinguish yin and yang is based on the density of energy in your body. High density of energy is called zhuo 濁, and low density of energy is called qing 清. Zhuo energy is descending energy, and accordingly it is yin. Qing energy is rising energy, and so it is yang. Yin and yang can not be separated. Yin nurtures yang, and yang nurtures yin. They are mixed together in your body.

It is sometimes difficult to say what is yin and what is yang, because where there is yin there is yang, and where there is

31

yang there is yin. They are together in one. It is important for taichi practitioners to remember that yin and yang are constantly in flux as they adjust to each other. You should never be limited by words.

二要論（陰陽）

天地間森羅萬象，新陳代謝，未有往而不復者，亦未有直而無曲者，蓋物有對峙，勢有回還，古今不易之理也。

嘗有世之論拳者，而兼論氣者矣。夫氣主于一，何分為二？所謂二者，即呼吸也，呼吸即陰陽也。拳不能無動靜，氣不能無呼吸，吸則為陰，呼則為陽。主乎靜者為陰，主乎動者為陽。上升為陽，下降為陰。陽氣上升而為陽，陽氣下行而為陰；陰氣下行為陰，陰氣上升即為陽，此陰陽之分也。何謂清濁？升而上者為清，降而下者為濁；清氣上升，濁氣下降；清者為陽，濁者為陰，陽以滋陰，陰以滋陽。渾而言之統為一氣，氣不能無陰陽，即所謂人不能無動靜，鼻不能無呼吸，口不能無出入。此謂循環不易之理也。

然而氣分為二，實在于一。有志于斯途者，慎勿以是為拘拘焉。

32

Third Essential Theory
Triple Classification of the Body

Energy travels throughout your whole body. And there are many parts in your body. It is not necessary to talk about every one of them. In taichi, the body, head, and torso are divided into top, middle, and bottom sections, while the extremities are divided into root, middle, and tip sections. These charts show the classification:

Part	Top	Middle	Bottom
Body	Head	Torso	Legs
Head	Forehead	Nose	Lower jaw
Torso	Chest	Stomach	Abdomen

Part	Root	Middle	Tip
Legs	Hips	Knees	Feet
Arms	Shoulders	Elbows	Hands
Hands	Wrists	Palms	Fingers

This is a general classification for talking about body parts, except for the feet. It is very important for taichi practitioners to know about this classification. When practicing you should start your movement from the bottom or tip section of the part, continue to the middle or center section, and at the same time apply the energy of the movement from the top or root section. If you do it incorrectly, the movement will be unfocused. Your movement will then lack clear direction or power, or it will be askew.

It is important to understand the function of these three sections of your body parts, but do not forget that the whole body from the top of your head to the bottom of your feet also must function as one. Always keep your body straight when you do taichi.

三要論 （三節）

夫氣本諸身，而身之節部甚繁，若逐節論之則違乎拳術宗旨。惟分三節而論，三節者，上、中、下，或根、中、梢也。

以一身而言：頭為上節，身為中節，腿為下節。
以頭言之：額為上節，鼻為中節，下頜為下節。
以身言之：胸為上節，腹為中節，丹田為下節。
以腿言之：足為梢節，膝為中節，胯為根節。
以臂言之：手為梢節，肘為中節，肩為根節。
以手言之：指為梢節，掌為中節，腕為根節。

節觀于此，而足不必論矣。然而自頂至足，莫不各有三節。要之，若無三節之分，即無著意之處。蓋上節不明，無依無宗；中節不明，渾身是空；下節不明，動輒跌傾。由此觀之，三節之論，豈可忽耶！

至于氣之發動，要從梢節領起，中節隨之，根節催之而已。然此乃節節分而言之者也。若合而言之，則上自頭頂，下至足底，四肢百骸，總為一節，夫何三節之有哉！又何謂三節中之各有三節雲乎哉！

Fourth Essential Theory
The Four Energy Tips

Now that we have discussed the body and energy, we talk about the four energy tips of your body. The four energy tips are easily overlooked by taichi practitioners, but they are important.

When your internal energy moves, it should go from inside to outside. Only then can you use it. If energy does not move from inside to the energy tips of your body, it has no power. And your activity is then mere exercise, not taichi. Energy should travel through your energy channels towards the tips. Otherwise, your movement will have no strength. If it does not travel all the way to the tips, then you will still lack strength. Therefore, it is important to understand these four tips in your body. What are they? They are:

1) Hair: According to Chinese medicine, hair is the tip of your blood circulatory system. Even though hair is not one of the five primary elements (metal, wood, water, fire, earth), and is not really connected with your arms and legs, the circulation of your blood ends in your hair, and energy originates in blood. Without blood, energy cannot travel at all, and certainly cannot travel to the tips of the energy channels. If the energy travels all the way to the hair at the top of your head, you feel as if your hair is sticking out against your hat, and then you know that there is plenty of energy in your blood.

2) Tongue: According to Chinese medicine, your tongue is the tip of your muscular system. Muscles are the carriers of the energy in your body. If energy cannot travel to the tongue, then the motion of your energy is powerless. If you feel your tongue is actually pressing against your upper teeth, you know there is plenty of energy in your muscles.

Chapter 4 Traditional Zhao Bao Tai Chi Theory

3) Teeth, and 4) Nails: According to Chinese medicine, teeth and nails are the tips of your skeleton. Teeth are the tips of your bones, and fingernails and toenails are the tips of your tendons. Energy travels through bones, tendons, and muscles to your teeth and nails. If you feel your teeth are so strong that they can almost chew on a piece of tendon, and your nails are so strong that they can almost break a bone, then you know there is plenty of energy in your body.

If there is plenty of energy in the four tips of your body, your movements are powerful and solid, and you can better control the motion of your energy. In push-hands, you can better understand the amount of strength with which you push, and you can apply your energy to your movement wisely.

四要論 （四梢）

試于論身論氣之外，而進論四梢者也。夫四梢者，身之余緒也。言身者初不及此，言氣者亦所罕聞。

然拳以由内而發于外，氣由身而達梢，故氣之用，不本諸身則虛而不實，不行諸梢則實而仍虛。梢豈可不講，然若論手足之指為梢，此特身之梢耳，而猶未及乎氣之梢也。四梢為何？

發，其一也。夫發之所系，不列于五行，無關乎四體，似不足論矣。然發為血之梢，血為氣之海，縱不必本諸發以論氣，要不可離乎血而生氣，不離乎血，即不得不兼乎發。發欲冲冠，血梢足矣。舌為肉之梢，而肉為氣之囊，氣不能行諸肉之梢，即無以充其氣之量。故必舌欲摧齒，而后肉梢方可足矣！至于骨梢者，齒也；筋梢者，指甲也。氣生于骨而聯于筋，不及乎齒，即未近乎骨之梢

Chapter 4 Traditional Zhao Bao Tai Chi Theory

不及乎指甲，亦未近乎筋之梢，而欲足四梢者，要非齒欲斷筋，甲欲透骨不能也。果能如此，則四梢足矣。四梢足而氣自足矣！豈復有虛而不實，實而仍虛之弊乎！

Fifth Essential Theory
The Five Primary Elements

Chinese medicine talks about the five primary elements: metal, wood, water, fire, and earth. They are associated with the five internal organs: lungs, liver, kidneys, heart, and spleen respectively. This is also what many taichi practitioners believe. They believe that these five organs are closely related to the quality of energy in your body.

Many taichi practitioners believe: 1) The heart is associated with fire. It is shaped like a flame, and it is the center where energy starts. 2) The liver is associated with wood. It is not shaped like a tree, but it is the largest gland in your body and it has straight and curved parts. 3) The spleen is associated with earth. It does not move very much. 4) The lungs are associated with metal. They breathe air and make noises. 5) The kidneys are associated with water. They nourish your reproductive system. Together these organs function as the main source of your life and create energy in your body. As a taichi practitioner, it is important for you to learn the positions of these five internal organs in your body.

Your lungs are in your chest. They protect your heart like an umbrella. When your diaphragm moves below your lungs, your lungs breathe, and then the other organs can get the oxygen that allows them to function.

Your heart is located in the middle of your chest. It is partly covered by your lungs. Your heart is above your diaphragm and is connected to your lungs on both sides. When your heart

Chapter 4 Traditional Zhao Bao Tai Chi Theory

contracts, it pumps blood that carries oxygen to other organs, and they function along with your heart like soldiers acting according to the orders of a king.

In between your ribs and below your diaphragm, your liver is on the right, your spleen is on the left, and your kidneys are by the middle of your backbone, one on each side at your waist. The blood vessels of your heart, lungs, liver, spleen, and kidneys are all connected with your backbone. Marrow is inside the bones of your backbone. Your kidneys perform the very important function of filtering wastes from your blood. If your kidneys have enough water to perform this function well, then the other organs can function well. These five internal organs in your body function differently, but they all depend on each other.

If you dissect a body, you will see the heart slightly protruding from between the lungs, the kidneys below the ribs, and the liver and spleen behind the abdominal muscles. Many taichi practitioners believe that there are relationships between your internal organs and aspects of taichi. Your heart is powerful like a tiger. Your liver is precipitous like an arrow. Your spleen is associated with courage and strength. Your lungs are associated with the changes of yin and yang because they inhale and exhale. And your kidneys are associated with the speed of your motion. As a taichi practitioner, through exercise and practice you can come to learn about these associations by feeling them in your body. It cannot all be explained in words.

五要論（五行）

夫拳以言勢，勢以言氣。人得五臟以成形，即由五臟而生氣，五臟實為性命之源、生氣之本，而各為心、肝、脾、肺、腎是也。心為火，而有炎上之象；肝為木，而有曲直之形；脾為土，而有敦厚之勢；肺為金，而有從革之能；腎為水，而有潤下之功。此乃五臟之義，而必準之于氣者，以其各有所配合焉。

此所以論拳事者，不能離乎斯也。其在于內，胸膈為肺經之位也，而肺為五臟之華蓋，故肺經動而諸臟不能靜。兩乳之中為心，而肺包護之，肺之下、膈之上，心經之位也。心為君火，心火動而兩相火無不奉命合焉。而兩肋之間，左為肝，右為脾。脊背十四骨節下為腎，此固五臟之位也，然五臟皆系于背脊。脊又通全身之髓，故為腎所主，至于腰之兩側，則腎居之本位，而為先天之第一，尤為諸臟之根源。故腎水足而金、木、水、火、土莫不各顯生機焉，此乃五臟之位所使之然也。且五臟之存乎內者，各有其定位，而具于身者，亦自有所專屬。

大約身之所系：中者、凸者為心，窩者為肺，骨之露處皆為腎，筋之聯處皆為肝，肉之厚處皆為脾。象其意：心如猛虎肝如箭，脾氣力大甚無窮，肺經之位最靈變，腎氣之動快如風。其為用也，是在當局者自為體認，而非筆墨所能罄者也。

39

Sixth Essential Theory
Six Connections

Now that we have discussed the five internal organs, let's talk about the six connections. When profound practitioners do taichi, the body binds all parts together into one, and there is only one energy behind them. Connected parts move together. So you need to pay attention to the six connections of your body. In general, this is how they are classified.
The mind is connected with thought, breathing is connected with energy, and tendons are connected with bones. The mind is connected with thought, thought is connected with energy, and energy is connected with strength. These are all internal connections.

The hands are connected with the feet, the elbows are connected with the knees, and the shoulders are connected with the hips. The back is connected with the shoulders, the shoulders are connected with the elbows, and the elbows are connected with the hands. The waist is connected with the hips, the hips are connected with the knees, and the knees are connected with the feet. These are all external connections.

In my opinion, when a profound practitioner does taichi, the left hand is connected with the right foot, the left elbow is connected with the right knee, and the left shoulder is connected with the right hip. The same is true on the other side of the body. The head is connected with the hands, the hands are connected with the torso, and the torso is connected with the legs. These are all external connections.

The mind is connected with the eyes, the liver is connected with the tendons, and the spleen is connected with the muscles. The lungs are connected with the torso, and the kidneys are connected with the backbone. These are internal connections. Ultimately, the body binds all parts together into one. When a profound practitioner starts to move, every part starts to move together in unison, and when the body stops moving, every part stops together. Everything in the whole body is unified.

六要論（六合）

五臟既明，再論六合。夫所謂"六合"者：心與意合，氣與力合，筋與骨合，是為"內三合"；亦有"心與意合，意與氣合，氣與力合"之"內三合"說。手與足合，肘與膝合，肩與胯合，是為"外三合"；又有"背與肩合，肩與肘合，肘與手合；腰與胯合，胯與膝合，膝與足合"的從上肢至下肢順序之"外三合"。上述皆為"六合"說。

若以左手與右足相合，左肘與右膝相合，左肩與右胯相合；右之與左亦然。

以及頭與手合，手與身合，身與步合，孰非外合？心與目合，肝與筋合，脾與肉合，肺與身合，腎與骨合；孰非內合？總之，一動而無有不動，一合而無有不合，五臟百骸悉在其中矣。

41

Chapter 4 Traditional Zhao Bao Tai Chi Theory

Seventh Essential Theory
Seven Active Movements

Now that we understand the six connections of your body, let's talk about the seven active movements of your body. They are movements of your head, hands, shoulders, upper arms, waist, feet, and torso.

Your head is the leader and commander of your body. When you take an action, your head moves. Your hands are the vanguard of your movement. Both of them always move. Your upper arms are the roots of your hands. If they do not move, your hands cannot move. Therefore, your upper arms must move. Of course, your upper arms are connected with your shoulders. So your shoulders must move.

When you move your hands, the energy gathers in your wrists. Because energy comes from your waist, if you do not move your waist, you will not have full energy in your hands. So it is necessary for you to move your waist.

Even though your mind controls your motion, to change your position your movement depends on your feet. If your feet stay in one place without moving, there is nothing your mind can do. So your feet have to move. To strike on the right, move your left foot. To strike on the left, move your right foot. Your torso is the pillar of your body. It holds every other part of your body together. Without moving your torso, you will be powerless.

These are the seven active movements of your body at the points at which you apply force. The key concept is that if none of them is moving, then nothing should be moving at all. When you decide to move them, none of them should be left behind. This is the principal of the seven active movements of your

Chapter 4 Traditional Zhao Bao Tai Chi Theory

body in taichi, push-hands, and combat. And that is all.

七要論 （七進）

既知六合，必知七進；頭為諸陽之首，而為周身之主，五官百骸，莫不惟首是瞻，故頭不可不進也；手為先鋒，根基在膊，膊不進則手不能前矣，故膊亦不可不進也；氣聚于腕，機關在腰，腰不進則氣餒而不實矣，此所以腰貴于進也；意貫周身，運動在步，步不進則意索然而無能為矣，此所以步必取其進也；以及上左必進右，上右必進左，則身為總柱，身不進則肢體散亂而無力，故身不可不進也。

此七進者，孰非着力之地歟？要之，未及其進，合周身而毫無關動之意；一言其進，統全體俱無抽扯游移之形。七進之道，如是而已矣。

43

Chapter 4 Traditional Zhao Bao Tai Chi Theory

Eighth Essential Theory
Eight Body Maneuvers

In combat, striking your opponent successfully depends on the eight techniques of maneuvering your body. What are they? They are:

   Extending the energy in your body
   Wrapping the energy in your body
   Elongating your body to make it taller
   Shrinking your body to make it shorter
   Taking a step forward
   Taking a step backward
   Turning your body to face the opposite direction
   Turning your body left or right

Extending the energy in your body means letting your energy go forward like the thrust of a wave hitting a beach, so that no one can stop it. Wrapping the energy in your body means holding your energy like the wide-open receding of a wave. Again, no one can stop it. Elongating your body to make it taller means holding your head upright like a tiger ready to attack, and extending your backbone as if you are growing taller. Shrinking your body to make it shorter means constricting your backbone as if you are sinking into water and growing shorter.

When you decide to take a step forward to strike, do not hesitate. Release all your energy. When you decide to take a step backward, hold your energy and prepare to turn and strike back with more energy. If you turn your body to face the opposite direction and look at that direction, then your back becomes your front. If you turn your body left or right and look toward that direction, then your left and right sides turn with you. Left or right is not an issue if you know your position.

Chapter 4 Traditional Zhao Bao Tai Chi Theory

In combat, it is very important to observe the strength and skill of your opponent, so you know how to apply your techniques wisely. There are no rules to follow exactly. You may suddenly decide to extend your energy or wrap your energy according to the changing situation. You may elongate or shrink your body when the time is right. Do not limit yourself to what the rules say. When it is time for you to step forward, you should not step backward and lose your advantage. When it is time for you to step backward, you should do so and wait for the opportunity to move forward. Therefore, you may step back with the strategy of moving forward. You are actually preparing to move forward and getting ready to strike your opponent. In combat, if you turn your body and face the opposite direction, do not think of the new direction as the opposite direction. If you turn your body left or right and look toward that direction, then your original left is no longer your left, and your original right is no longer your right.

After all, the keys to winning in combat are the observation of your eyes and the flexibility of your mind for changing your position. You should remember these eight techniques of maneuvering your whole body. When your body moves forward, all parts of your body automatically move forward together. When your body moves backward, all parts of your body move backward together. These eight techniques of maneuvering your whole body are so important. How can we not talk about them?

八要論（身法）

　　夫發手擊敵，全賴身法之助。身法惟何？縱橫高低進退反側而已。縱，則放其勢，一往而不返。橫，則裹其力，開拓而莫阻。高，則揚其身，而身若有增長之意。低，則抑其身，而身若有攢促之形。當進則進，殫其力而勇往直前；當退則退，束其氣而回轉扶勢。　至于反身顧后，后即前也；側顧左右，左右安敢當我哉！而非拘拘焉為之也。

　　察乎人之強弱，運乎己之機關。有忽縱而忽橫，縱橫因勢而變遷，不可一概而推之；有忽高而忽低，高低隨時以轉移，不可執格而論。時而宜進，故不可退而餒其氣；時而宜退，即當以退而鼓其進。是退固進也，即退而實以蘊其進。若反身顧后，而后亦不覺其為后；側顧左右，而左右亦不覺其為左右矣。

　　總之，機關在眼，變通在心，而握其要者，則本諸身。身而前，則四體不命而行矣；身而卻，則百骸莫不冥然而處矣。身法，豈可置而不論乎？

Ninth Essential Theory
Techniques of Stepping

Human bodies are made to move. And moving depends on your feet. When you walk, you simply step forward in the direction you are facing, but when you do tai chi, you have to learn the techniques of stepping. Only then can you win in combat. Stepping is like the turning of a car's tires. It gets you where you want to go.

In combat, you change the movement of your hands according to the situation. But the movements of your feet go together with the movements of your hands. Without properly moving your feet to take a step, you cannot move your body forward, move your body backward, turn your body to face the opposite direction, or turn your body left or right; and you cannot effectively extend the energy in your body, wrap the energy in your body, elongate your body to make it taller, or shrink your body to make it shorter. The keys to winning in combat are the observation of your eyes and the flexibility of your mind, but how far you turn your body and the direction to which you turn both depend on your footwork. Your movements may not work for you if you just step in any way you wish.

It is very important for you as a tai chi practitioner to understand that you should make every movement naturally and without force. It is as if you do not even think about it. You should apply your energy naturally, as if you are not even aware of it. Before your body moves, your feet already start to step out. Before your hands move, your feet already send energy to your hands. It happens without planning. You make a step without consciously willing it. When the upper body

Chapter 4 Traditional Zhao Bao Tai Chi Theory

moves, the lower body is already following. This is what is meant by the techniques of stepping.

There are rules for the techniques of stepping. When you practice tai chi, one rule is that you generally step to put one foot in front of the other at a 45° angle. But in combat, you may break this rule. Another rule is that if your front foot moves, your back foot should follow. If you step back so that your front foot goes in back of your back foot, then your original back foot becomes your new front foot, and your original front foot becomes your new back foot. In other cases, even after you step back, your front foot can still be in front of your back foot, and even after you step forward, your back foot can still be in back of your front foot. Therefore, there is no certain rule about which foot is in front or which foot is in back.

In general, it is very important for the tai chi practitioner to understand the techniques of stepping. The way you step determines whether your body movements are lively or not. It also determines the flexibility of your mind. It also determines your effectiveness in combat.

九要論 （步法）

夫四肢百骸主于動，而實運之以步。步乃一身之根基，運動之樞紐也。以故應戰對敵，本諸身，而所以為身之砥柱者，莫非步也。隨機應變在于手，而所以為手之轉移者，亦在于步。進退反側，非步何以作鼓蕩之機？抑揚伸縮，非步何以示變化之妙？所謂機關在眼，變化在心；而轉彎抹角，千變萬化，不至于窘迫者何？莫非步為之司命歟？而非勉強以致之也。

動作出于無心，鼓舞出于不覺，身欲動而步已為之周旋，手將動而步亦早為之催逼，不期然而已然，莫之驅而若驅，所謂"上欲動而下自隨之者"，其斯之謂歟？且步分前後，有定位者，步也；無定位者，亦步也！如前步進，而后步亦隨之，前後自有定位。若以前步作後步，後步作前步；更以前步作後步之前步，后步作前步之後步，則前后亦自無定位矣。

總之，拳以論勢，而握其要者，步也；活與不活在于步，靈與不靈亦在于步，步之為用大矣哉！

Tenth Essential Theory
Hard and Soft Energy

The nine essential theories already discussed are the foundation of tai chi. Why is this? It is because they are basic to the application of tai chi. And the basis of the application of tai chi is how you move your energy inside your body and how you apply that energy outside your body. The energy inside your body may be fierce or gentle, and the energy your apply outside your body may be hard or soft. People who have a lot of internal energy usually apply external energy that is hard like a tiger's. A strong, profound martial arts practitioner uses one thousand pounds of energy to take down someone who has one hundred pounds of energy. A profound tai chi practitioner who may have less internal energy usually applies external energy that is quite soft. But with skill, he or she may use one hundred pounds of energy to take down someone who has one thousand pounds of energy. With strength or skill, you see the difference in tai chi between hardness and softness.

There is a difference between hard energy and soft energy. They are different in their applications. You may see someone who appears full of impending doom inside and full of energy outside. That is hard energy. Or you may see someone who appears full of energy inside, but outside looks gentle and relaxed. That is soft energy. In combat, when you strike your opponent vigorously, it is necessary to have soft energy inside your body. Without soft energy inside, your strike can not spiral fast enough. But it is also important to have some hard energy inside your soft movement before you strike your opponent. Without hard energy you can notfollow your opponent's energy fast enough. Soft energy is yin and hard

Chapter 4 Traditional Zhao Bao Tai Chi Theory

energy is yang, and yin and yang are constantly in flux as they adjust to each other.

There are twenty techniques for using the hands and upper body in Zhaobao Taichi Kungfu. They are:

1) 粘 zhān : To glue your energy to your opponent.
2) 连 lián: To connect your energy with your opponent.
3) 黏 nián : To be glued to your opponent with your energy.
4) 随 suí : To follow your opponent's energy.
5) 腾 téng: To raise your energy going straight towards your opponent.
6) 闪 shǎn: To raise your energy going sideways towards your opponent.
7) 拆 chāi: To avoid your opponent's energy that coming straight towards you.
8) 空 kōng: To avoid your opponent's energy that coming sideways towards you.
9) 掤 péng : To block your opponent's energy.
10) 捋 lǚ : To twist your arms and lead your opponent's energy in a different direction.
11) 挤 jǐ : To press your energy in your hands towards your opponent.
12) 按 àn : To push one or both of your hands and spiral your arm or arms downward onto your opponent's energy.
13) 採 cǎi: To lock your opponent's wrist inward, and pull his or her elbow up.
14) 挒 liè : To lock your opponent's wrist outward, and pull his or her elbow down.

51

Chapter 4 Traditional Zhao Bao Tai Chi Theory

15) 肘 zhǒu: To strike your opponent with your elbow.
16) 靠 kào: To strike your opponent with your shoulder.
17) 缠 chán: To grip your opponent's hand or arm, and twist it in a small circle.
18) 绕 rào: To grip your opponent's hand or arm, and twist it in a big circle.
19) 背 bēi : To lock your opponent's wrist, turn your body, and pull your opponent's elbow to throw him or her over your shoulder.
20) 打 dǎ: To strike your opponent with your head, shoulders, elbows, or knees.

These twenty techniques of the hands and upper body in Zhaobao Taichi Kungfu should be applied naturally and with correct proportions of hard and soft energy. In combat, too much soft energy or too much hard energy is not effective. This is very important for a tai chi practitioner to keep in mind. A profound tai chi practitioner uses many widely varied techniques, but the basic principles are always to keep the body straight and upright, and to keep movements even and circular. These are also the principles that sages and virtuous people use to conduct themselves in life.

Chapter 4 Traditional Zhao Bao Tai Chi Theory

十要論（剛柔）

　　綜上九要，乃拳術之本也；本者何？乃拳術之體用也。夫拳術之為用，氣與勢而已矣！然而氣有強弱，勢分剛柔。氣強者取乎勢之剛，氣弱者取乎勢之柔。剛者以千鈞之力而扼百鈞之力；柔者以百鈞之力而破千鈞之力。尚力尚巧，剛柔之所以分也！

　　然則剛柔即分，而發用亦自有別；四肢發動，氣行于外而內持靜重，剛勢也；氣屯于內而外顯輕和，柔勢也；用剛不可無柔，無柔則環繞不速；用柔不可無剛，無剛則催逼不捷。剛柔相濟，則粘、連、黏、隨、騰、閃、拆、空、掤、挒、擠、按、採、捯、肘、靠、纏、繞、背、打，無不得其自然矣！剛柔不可偏用，用武者豈可忽略耶！

　　拳術之體，大矣廣矣；或言中、正、平、圓，此乃聖賢立世之本也。

Chapter 4 Traditional Zhao Bao Tai Chi Theory

3. The Five Skill Levels of Zhaobao Taichi Kungfu

The history of Chinese martial arts is long. There have been many different schools in the past and present. While each school has its own characteristics, Zhaobao Taichi Kungfu is one of the outstanding schools of them all. Zhaobao Taichi's movements are not only artistic exercises for health and effective self-defense skills, but also a way of expressing the essence of traditional culture and philosophy through body movement. Its movements show the deepest ancient philosophy. Practicing Zhaobao Taichi Kungfu not only benefits one's health, but also cultivates one's mind. In the end, it is the practice of reaching the highest potential in one's life.

The five skill levels of Zhaobao Taichi Kungfu are:

形 xíng (appearance): Understanding basic taichi movements and their applications

法 fǎ (learning): Changing the body's positions and listening to internal energy

知 zhī (awareness): Being aware of one's limited situation

理 lǐ (principle): Harmonizing oneself with nature

化 huà (change): Transcending one's energy and uniting oneself with nature

Xíng is the elementary level of Zhaobao Taichi Kungfu. Huà is the highest level of Zhaobao Taichi Kungfu. At the huà level, one's body has reached the state of transcendence, and one's skill and mind have matured.

Chapter 4 Traditional Zhao Bao Tai Chi Theory

The Xíng Level
The Xing level is expressed by Zhaobao Taichi practitioners with the proverb:

Qǐluòxiánshú,
Chūshǒujiàngōng

The Chinese characters are: 起落娴熟,出手見功. The literal translation of these terms is: Rising, falling, skillful, experienced; extend, hand, see, result. A loose translation is:

Through rising and falling, become skillful and experienced;
Extending the hand, see the result.

When one's taichi skill has reached the elementary xíng level, one has developed an understanding of internal energy. Qǐluòxiánshú means that one has begun to become familiar with the ups and downs of the taichi movements, the framework of internal energy, and the forms of routine taichi exercises. Chūshǒujiàngōng means that one has begun to understand how to apply one's internal energy for the purpose of self-defense in combat.

The Fǎ Level
The fǎ level is the level of entering the inner hall of the world of taichi. It is expressed by Zhaobao Taichi practitioners with the proverb:

Huídāngzhuǎnhuàn,
Cǎiqìjùtīng

The Chinese characters are: 回襠轉換，采氣聚聽. The literal translation of these terms is: Return, crotch, turn, change; gather, energy, concentrate, listen. Knowing how to move the torso and change the position;

Chapter 4 Traditional Zhao Bao Tai Chi Theory

A loose translation is:

> Knowing how to move the torso and change the position;
> Gathering energy and be sensitive in listening.

It means that one is at the level of extending one's skills from the hands and legs to the whole body, and that one's whole body has become sensitive to movement.

Huídāngzhuǎnhuàn means that one has understood how to move the torso together with the fist or hand. The purpose is to shift the weight in combat in order to face attack from all directions. The whole body turns on the axis of the hips, like a wheel that can turn in any direction. The opponent then unable to attack. Cǎiqìjùtīng means that one is sensitive to body movement, feelings, and surroundings. A taichi proverb says: Collect spirit from heaven and earth; gather energy from the sun and moon. This saying suns up the sensitivity of the taichi practitioner's body to the energy field of his or her surroundings.

The Zhī Level

The zhī level is expressed by ZhaoBao Taichi practitioners with the proverb:

> Kànguāndǐngjiè,
> Zhīdùérmíng

The Chinese characters are: 看關頂戒, 知度而明. The literal translation of these terms is: Observe, close up, oppose, abstain from; aware of, limit, and, understand. A loose translation is:

> Observing the opponent and closing up his/her retreat, put caution first;
> Being aware of one's limits, understand the situation.

Chapter 4 Traditional Zhao Bao Tai Chi Theory

The zhī level is the level at which one has entered the secret realm of taichi, and has reached the crucial time of becoming a master. Kàn means paying attention to the opponent's attack, and at the same time being aware of one's defense; guān means closing up the opponent's retreat; dǐng means blocking the movement of the attack from the opponent; and jiè means keeping one's mind in the best state, without making mistakes. Zhīdùérmíng means not overreacting to the attack, keeping one's mind and body upright, being aware of one's limits, and understanding the situation.

The Lǐ Level

The lǐ level is the level at which one has become a master in taichi. It is expressed by ZhaoBao Taichi practitioners with the proverb:

Yǐtiānfǎrén,
Jìcóngdàoshēng

The Chinese characters are: 以天法人，技從道生. The literal translation of these terms is: Use, nature, learn, people; skill, from, philosophy, born. A loose translation is:

Nature sets the pattern for a person;
Skills are born from philosophy.

The meaning of this proverb is that one understands the relationship between oneself as a person and the outside world of nature. One has united and harmonized oneself with nature. One is capable of moving the body naturally. One applies the Daoist philosophy of Laozi to one's gestures, and the Doctrine of the Mean to one's movements. One has extended one's skills and learned from this philosophy.

Chapter 4 Traditional Zhao Bao Tai Chi Theory

The Huà Level
The huà level is the level of completely absorbing the philosophy of the universe and uniting oneself with nature. It is expressed by Zhaobao Taichi practitioners with the proverb:
Yìsībúguà,
Wúzōngwúxíng
The Chinese characters are: 一丝不挂，无踪无形. The literal translation of these terms is: One, silk, not, hang; no, trace, no, appearance. A loose translation is:

> Transcending oneself without a piece of silk hanging;
> Uniting oneself with nature without any trace.

In one's movements at the huà level, do you see the energy or not? The highest skill seems ordinary. Nothing shows outside of the body, but the internal energy is moving there. Outside movements seem slow, but the internal energy moves fast. There is a saying in Chinese that one's skill is so skillful that it become ordinary. At this level of taichi, every movement one does is just right, without force. If you were to add the weight of a feather or a fly, it would be too much. One is so skillful that the opponent has no way of knowing what one is doing, but one knows exactly what the opponent is doing. One's whole body has transcended itself and one clearly understands the work of taichi. For a practitioner, this is the ultimate level. One has returned to nature and become part of nature. It is the truth of life and taichi.

3. 趙堡太極功夫之五層境界-宋蘊華

中華武術源遠流長，門類繁多，風格各異，趙堡太極拳更是武術叢林中的一枝奇葩。趙堡太極拳不僅是一種優秀的健身運動及搏擊防身技術，同時也是中國傳統文化的精華體現，其中蘊含了極深刻的哲理思想，所以它不但修身而且養性，最終是一種人生境界的修煉。

趙堡太極功夫講求五層境界，即：**形、法、知、理、化**。形界為初級入門階段；化界是全體透空、爐火純青的最高階段。

形界：起落嫻熟、出手見功

形界的八字口訣是："起落嫻熟，出手見功"。此謂太極功夫鍛煉已達入門階段，并在和對方交手時已基本具備太極勁兒。"起落嫻熟"是指太極拳功架、行拳已初步完善，熟練程度可想而知。"出手見功"是指打手搏擊已初步掌握力道。

法界：回襠轉換、采氣聚聽

法界是登堂階段："回襠轉換，采氣聚聽"即謂手腳功夫已開始上升為身上功夫，皮膚及肢體感覺靈敏。"回襠轉換"也就是拳手能用襠胯調節重心，對付來自四面八方的打擊。全身以襠為軸心，像似一個萬向輪，旋轉不定，令對手無措難以攻擊。"采氣聚聽"就是耳聰目明和觸覺感應的抽象概念，所謂"采天地之靈氣，聚日月之精華"，包括了全身內外肢體觸覺和外部氣場感應。

知界：看關頂戒、知度而明

知界的八字口訣為"看關頂戒，知度而明"，是太極功夫的入室階段，也是一個拳師的關鍵時刻。"看關頂戒"包涵四個內容："看"是注意敵方來勢，同時包含看守自家的防護意識；"關"是關閉自己的穴位同時封鎖對手退路；"頂"是封住敵方實招；"戒"是指自己要有良好的意志品質和心理素質,不要犯心理上的錯誤。"知度而明"是指應招不能過分、保持中庸、掌握分寸，如果一旦越位，超越了這個"度"，必敗無疑。

理界：以天法人、技從道生

理界是成手階段，八字口訣為"以天法人，技從道生"。在哲學含義上指主觀與客觀的統一，所謂"天人合一"，"天人感應"，是要求搏擊手做到身體本能與自然的和諧與統一。其觀點是"以老子之道定拳勢，以中庸之道定拳風"的無限延伸。達到如此境界，即為宗師。

化界：一絲不挂、無踪無形

化界是完全哲學化了的境界。其八字訣為"一絲不挂,無踪無形"。其中有物？還是其中無物？大巧若拙，外靜內動。外慢內快，所謂"心機入妙，終歸無心"。太極功夫練到如此境界，"一羽不能加，蠅蟲不能落；人不知我，我獨知人，全體透空，契機通明"。這是練功習武之人大道歸一的超境界之境界；即為返璞歸真。

Chapter 4 Traditional Zhao Bao Tai Chi Theory

4. The Five Primary Elements and the Eight Body Maneuvers of Zhaobao Taichi

Although the five primary elements of traditional Chinese medicine and philosophy are metal, wood, water, fire, and earth, Zhaobao Taichi also refers to its five basic fighting techniques as the five primary elements. They are: zhān, rào, bēi, jìn, jí. Applying these five primary elements is the fundamental principle of combat strategy.

1) Zhān is gluing. You glue your energy to your opponent's energy with your hand, and bring yourself close to your opponent. After all, tai chi is an art form of close combat, so engaging with your opponent is to your advantage.

2) Rào is spiraling. In combat, after you connect your energy with your opponent's and he or she strikes you, you spiral your energy to escape, or you spiral your opponent's energy in a circle to make him or her lose balance.

3) Bēi is shouldering. It means carrying something on your back. After you connect your energy with your opponent's, you move his or her center of gravity to your shoulder and make him or her lose balance, and then twist his or her forearm. This technique is commonly used by Zhaobao Taichi practitioners.

4) Jìn is stepping. Without stepping, you can not properly glue your energy to your opponent's. It is then difficult for you to strike. Stepping makes striking easier.

5) Jí is striking. In combat, you may strike your opponent with your hand, fist, foot, knee, hip, elbow, or shoulder. If you are close enough to your opponent, you may strike your opponent with your knee or elbow. If you are more distant, then you should strike him or her with your foot or hand.

61

Chapter 4 Traditional Zhao Bao Tai Chi Theory

There is a poem that describes the five primary elements of Zhaobao Taichi Kungfu. It is:
> You must remember zhān, rào, bēi, jìn, jí;
> They are profound, and rare in our world.
> Even if you only know a third of the art,
> You know how to come and go through the gate of life and death.

What Zhaobao Taichi Kungfu traditionally refers to as the eight body maneuvers is actually three sets of eight maneuvers each, for a total of 24. They are: 1) yǐn, lǐng, suǒ, kòu, lāo, guà, lóu, fān; 2) tūn, tǔ, kāi, hé, xuán, bǎi, zòng, héng; and 3) chán, guì, tiǎo, liào, tiē, cuò, dèng, chuài.

1) Eight hand maneuvers:
• Yǐn means you let your energy be glued to your opponent's energy, and at the same time you drive his or her energy into a disadvantageous position.

• Lǐng means you glue the energy in your hand to your opponent's energy, and at the same time drive his or her energy into a disadvantageous position.

• Suǒ means you grasp the energy in your opponent's hand or arm with your hand.

• Kòu means you lock your opponent's forearm or weapon with your hand, making him or her unable to escape for a instant so that you may immediately strike him or her.

• Lāo means you put one hand palm down on your opponent's wrist and the other hand palm up on his or her elbow, and lift the elbow up.

Guà means you hook your hand on your opponent's forearm to grasp him or her.

• Lóu means you grasp your opponent's waist with your hands, with your thumbs up or down.

Chapter 4 Traditional Zhao Bao Tai Chi Theory

• Fān means you lift up your opponent's arm with your two hands, and you combine the energy of your hands.

2) Eight hip maneuvers:
• Tūn means you twist your hips in a figure eight pattern to dissolve your opponent's energy as it comes towards you.
• Tǔ means you strike your opponent with your hips upwards at a 45° angle to make him or her lose balance.
• Kāi means you open your groin and divide your energy into two directions to trap your opponent's energy inside your energy.
• Hé means you close your groin and make your energy descend to defend yourself.
• Xuán means you spiral your hips evenly to trap your opponent in front of your chest.
• Bǎi means you twist your hips to the left or right in order to strike the center of your opponent's body.
• Zòng means you use your hips to strike your opponent, going straight towards him or her before you take him or her down.
• Héng means you use your hips to strike your opponent who is coming towards you from your side.

3) Eight leg or foot maneuvers:
• Chán means you turn your leg inward to twist your opponent's front leg.
• Guì means you use your knee to drive your opponent's front leg down.
• Tiǎo means you walk straight towards your opponent and use your front foot to twist his or her front ankle outwards.
• Liào means you strike your opponent with your thigh and raise his or her feet up off the ground.

Chapter 4 Traditional Zhao Bao Tai Chi Theory

- Tiē means you contact your opponent's thigh with your thigh by twisting your hip.
- Cuò means you thrust your leg sideways in a shoveling motion so your foot forces your opponent's calf or knee downward, outward, and then upward. Or you curl your toes to grip the ground so you keep your balance.
- Dèng means you strike your opponent with your heel going straight towards him or her.
- Chuài means you strike your opponent at your side using the sole or side of your foot, with your head down and one leg up.

There is a poem that describes how powerful the eight maneuvers of Zhaobao Taichi Kungfu are. It goes like this:

> The eight maneuvers are powerful in tai chi;
> Hands, legs, and hips, you use them all.
> When they appear, they shock the skies;
> When they are hidden, they provide good defense.
> With them, striking your opponent becomes easy;
> Every maneuver is killing.
> When you decide to strike, you are like a demon of hell.
> But when you are calm, you are like a living Buddha.

4. 趙堡太極五行八法論-宋蘊華

五行總訣
粘、繞、背、進、擊
歌訣
牢記粘繞背進擊，此種絕技世間稀，
倘若識得三分藝，生死門中知來去。

五行乃周身之搏擊總訣，是戰略性之大綱。

粘，謂近身之技。太極拳屬短拳類，粘貼近戰是其優勢。

繞，周身受力時自繞，乃謂金蟬脫殼之技，受力時順勢讓對方翻滾相隨，乃謂作繭自縛之法。

背，趙堡太極拳慣用之法，背乃背物之背，受力時順勢將對方臂膊引重肩上，然后進行反關節背折打擊。

進，無進則粘不可及，無進則力不從心。進者，乃貼身近戰之妙也。

擊，即手掌、拳、腳、膝、胯、肘尖、肩頭進行擊打之技，"近了用膝肘，遠了用腳手"之謂也。

八法總訣
上八法
引、領、鎖、扣、撈、挂、摟、翻
中八法
吞、吐、開、合、旋、擺、縱、橫
下八法
纏、跪、挑、撂、貼、銼、蹬、踹

Chapter 4 Traditional Zhao Bao Tai Chi Theory

八法歌訣

太極神技有八法，手腿襠胯皆有他。
現身即為驚天技，收勢看門護自家。
出手制敵取人巧，招招奪命是絕殺。
動容猶如閻羅鬼，靜時好似活菩薩。

上、中、下八法，乃四梢之技，上、中、下共二十四種；此乃趙堡太極拳傳統打法。

上八法：引、領、鎖、扣、撈、挂、摟、翻。

引，受力時帶領對方于不利之地；領，無論受力與不受力、主動牽誘對方于不利之地；鎖，即拿死對方手、臂；扣，即用手按住對方手臂或器械，使其瞬間不能走脫，再伺機進行攻擊；撈，即是將對方沉肘弄起；挂，即用勾手搭住對方手臂；摟，近身以反或正之形式控制對方腰部；翻，將對方臂膊用合力之技術掀起。

中八法：吞、吐、開、合、旋、擺、縱、橫。

吞，襠胯迂回旋轉化掉對方之力；吐，襠胯跳彈而攻，使對方失重之技；開，襠胯向兩邊分，吃進對方；合，襠胯內收、下縮，看護自家；旋，襠胯平行旋轉，使對方正面受漁；擺，兩胯左右擺動，擊打對方中部；縱，襠胯正面跳進，主要用于擒拿；橫，襠胯側向跳進，擊打身側之敵。

Chapter 4　Traditional Zhao Bao Tai Chi Theory

下八法：纏、跪、挑、撂、貼、銼、蹬、踹。

纏，乃用腿繞住對方之腿；跪，即以膝跪方式打其腿關節；挑，即用腳撥起對方之腿；撂，即用腿將對方扔出；貼，即大腿在襠胯配合下緊貼對方大腿；銼，一是指用腳側鏟擊對方小腿或膝部，一是指用雙腳緊抓地面；蹬，乃用腳跟擊打之法；踹，即指用腳掌、腳側踢打之技。

Chapter 4 Traditional Zhao Bao Tai Chi Theory

5. The Fighting Techniques of Zhaobao Taichi Kungfu

Zhaobao Taichi kungfu is a school of taichi that combines three techniques in one. These three techniques are movements, push-hands, and san shou. The techniques are designed for health development, fighting, and self-defense. The movements are the foundation for health, and fighting and self-defense are further purposes.

The movements of Zhaobao Taichi kungfu are beautiful, graceful, soft, smooth, and natural. They look elegant, and they continuously change from one to another. The movements can be big or small, high or low, and fast or slow. It depends on what is natural for individuals. But there are a few principles that must be followed by practitioners. They are: 1) You must always keep your body straight and upright, so your movements can be even, circular, light, quick, soft, and lively. 2) You must move like a spinning wheel that is spinning silk to make a continuous silk thread. And your energy should move like a three-foot strip of gauzy silk hanging from a tree branch and swinging freely in the wind, weightless, without any physical limit and without a shadow. It should move like a river flowing smoothly or a cloud drifting lightly. It goes up or down and left or right, and it twists and turns in any direction. 3) Your body movements must be circular, and not in straight lines. This means your hands, arms, shoulders, hips, elbows, knees, and whole body all have to move in circles or curves, like your steps. You must reach the point at which your feet step in a circle, your hands move in a circle, your limbs twist in a circle, and your body moves in a circle. The whole set of movements should consist of many circles of turns and twists until you stop moving when you have completed the pattern. Although we use the term "circle," we really mean a series of

Chapter 4 Traditional Zhao Bao Tai Chi Theory

three-dimensional spheres put together one after another. The quality of these moving spheres is the basis and origin of the power in Zhaobao Taichi kungfu.

The basis of the fighting technique in Zhaobao Taichi kungfu is push-hands. San shou is the application of push-hands to fighting at a greater distance. And grappling is the application of push-hands to fighting at a smaller distance. Push-hands is good for testing the accuracy of your postures and movements. At the same time, movement exercises can help you to improve the level of your fighting techniques in push-hands and San shou.

The basic theory of push-hands in Zhaobao Taichi kungfu comes from *The Book of Changes*. Yin and yang are constantly in flux as they adjust to each other, and the changes of yin and yang are always present. Therefore, the fighting techniques of Zhaobao Taichi kungfu use softness to overcome the hard, weakness to conquer the strong, and stillness to control motion. Always remember these principles. Keep your body straight and upright, and your movements even and circular. Do not attack your opponent with force. Keep yourself in a position from which you can easily move left or right. Follow your opponent's energy without asserting anything of your own. In combat, search for the quality of your spheres. By keeping your body upright and your movements circular, you ensure that your center of gravity is well-balanced. Then apply your spheres vigorously to attract your opponent's energy to them, and counter your opponent's attack along a tangent line. Through centrifugal force, in the end your opponent will lose his or her balance, and fall. If you are able to stand straight as if you are carrying one thousand pounds of weight on your head, then you may see the

Chapter 4 Traditional Zhao Bao Tai Chi Theory

result of using four ounces of your strength to throw your opponent who attacks you with one thousands pounds of force. Thus, the real technique of push-hands is definitely not resisting by force. Rather, it is based on the quality of your spheres. In this way, Zhaobao Taichi kungfu brings the technique of push-hands into full play.

The traditional characteristics of Zhaobao Taichi kungfu are softness like cotton, hardness like steel, slipperiness like a fish, and stickiness like fish glue. You should have thoughts of using softness to overcome the hard, and weakness to conquer the strong. In push-hands exercise or in combat, if the movement of your opponent's energy is hard, yours should be soft. Attract your opponent's energy inwards and counter your opponent's attack along a tangent line. Harmonize your motion to the motion of your opponent and follow your opponent's motion as closely as if you were glued to him or her, and then strike before your opponent has an opportunity.

The meaning of pushing in push-hands includes degrees of pushing, forms of pushing, and theories of pushing. Practitioners say that pushing involves holding oneself still like a virgin, moving the body like a tiger, thinking fast like a running horse, moving the hands rapidly like the wind, twisting the torso like a falling wall, and stepping down with your feet like a tree putting down roots.

The strategies in combat are to think about moving, and never to retreat. Striking without moving your feet forward does not work. Rather, it is effective to step forward when your hand strikes. Do not show what you intend to do. If you show your intention, you will have no chance to win. If your opponent is far from you, then strike with your hands or legs; if your opponent is close to you, then strike with your knees or elbows. Contact your opponent as if you are carefully carrying a weight on your

Chapter 4 Traditional Zhao Bao Tai Chi Theory

shoulders, and when you strike, it should be as if you are casting the weight off from your shoulders. Hide your palm or back of your hand when your hand is in front of your chest. If your elbow is in front of your chest, it should be low as if you do not really see it. Your hands should be steady, but your feet should move lightly like a cat walking. Your mind should be focused and your eyes should be alert, so when you strike with your hands and feet moving together you will win. Never close your eyes in combat, so you can observe your opponent's expression and position. Your mind should be like gunpowder and your hands like a bullet; when you pull the trigger, it is impossible for a bird to fly away. When you strike in a high position, hit your opponent's throat. When you strike in low position, hit your opponent's crotch. Otherwise, strike your opponent's ribs on the left or right, or strike the middle of the chest. The distance between you and your opponent is not an issue, as it can be an inch away or many feet. Do not make a strike based on your opponent's ineffective or deceptive movements. The movements of your joints should be smooth, as otherwise they will be powerless. If you grapple with your opponent, do it vigorously so your opponent's position does not change. When you decide to strike, strike immediately, as any delay in your action can cause problems. And when you strike, the movement should be fast, so it can be more accurate. If you throw your opponent, do it wholeheartedly, so your attack can be powerful. Move your feet and hands vigorously, so there is no chance for your opponent to attack you. Your strategy should be profound, so you are not trapped by your opponent. Understand how energy is connected in your body, so when you move, the energy travels directly to your head from your dantian, the point inside your body three inches below your navel. If you understand the

Chapter 4 Traditional Zhao Bao Tai Chi Theory

connections of your body, you will have more strategies to work with. Your mind is the commander. Your energy is the element that makes your hands move up and down, and your feet move forwards and backwards. All of this takes a long time to understand, and it is necessary to practice day and night for a long period. In the beginning it is difficult, but in the end, it becomes your nature.

5. 趙堡太極拳技擊特點

趙堡太極拳是一套三合一的太極拳流派；即拳架、推手及散手三者合而為一也。簡單來說就是把養生、技擊和防身自衛融合在一起，以拳架為基礎，以技擊防身為應用。

趙堡太極拳拳架姿勢優美雅靜，柔順自然，儀態萬千，變化多端；其姿勢動作可大可小，可高可低；運動速度可快可慢，純任自然；但是練習此拳必須注意始終保持中、正、平、圓、輕、靈、柔、活的體態。動作如抽絲，大纏小纏，絲絲相連，感覺猶如三尺羅衣挂在無影樹頭，無軀干之限，隨風飄蕩，灑脫自如；行似流水，輕若浮雲，既有上下起伏，亦有左右翻騰，更有轉動八方之勢；運動要求走圓，不走直綫；身、手、步、肢、肩、胯、肘、膝都做圓形或弧形的轉動和滾動；做到步走圓周。手化圓周，身行圓周，肢繞圓周，而整個套路是經歷了無數次的內圈加外圈的轉動和滾動，才能完成；這些圓圈并不是停留在一個平面空間上，而是一個個立體的圓，一個個三維空間的圓；這些立體圓的質量，就是動力的基礎和源泉。

Chapter 4 Traditional Zhao Bao Tai Chi Theory

　　趙堡太極拳技擊的基本功主要是推手，散手是推手的延伸，而擒拿則是推手的近縮。推手可以用來檢查拳架姿勢動作是否準確，拳架也可以幫助提高推手、散手在實踐中的技擊水平。趙堡太極推手的理論基礎，是《易經》中的剛柔相濟，變在其中，所以趙堡太極拳技擊的特點是以柔克剛、以弱勝強、以靜制動，保持立身中、正、平、圓的原則，用招不硬上，出手必居正，一切圓滑自如，舍己從人。技擊時講求立體圓的質量，以中、正、平、圓來穩固自己的重心，靈活地運用立體圓，將對方引入自己立體圈的軌迹中，以圓的各個切面來化解對方的攻擊，在離心力的作用下，使對方重心動搖，站立不穩，從而跌倒，這就需要自身做到"立木頂千斤"，才能發揮到"四兩撥千斤"的效應。所以真正的太極推手技擊并不是拙力的抗衡，而是立體圓的較量，這個道理，在趙堡太極拳的推手技擊中，正好發揮得淋灕盡致。

　　趙堡太極拳的傳統特點是"軟如棉、硬如剛、滑如魚、粘如鰾"，并能達到以柔克剛，以弱勝強，避實就虛，引進落空，逆來順受，以順制逆，后發制人的搏擊思想。推手之"推"，有推度、推演、推理的含義；正所謂：不動若處子，動則如猛虎，心動快似馬，手動速如風，身動如牆倒，腳落樹栽根；能叫一思進，莫叫一思退；手到步不到，打人不得妙；手到步亦到，打人如薅草；有意莫帶形，帶形必不贏；遠了用腳手，近了加膝肘；出手如擔擔，打人如卸肩；面前有手不見手，胸前有肘不見肘；手要穩、足要輕，

73

Chapter 4 Traditional Zhao Bao Tai Chi Theory

把式走動如貓行；心要整、目要精，手足齊發自然贏；睜眼吉、閉眼凶，察顏審勢我自明；心如火藥手如子，靈機一動鳥難飛；上打咽喉，下打陰，左右兩肋中打心；前打一丈不為遠，近打只在一寸間；見空不打，見詐不打；骨節要順，不順則無力；手把要靈，不靈則生變；起手要快，不快則遲誤；拳手要火，不火則不準；打手要狠，不狠則失威；腳手要活，不活則擔險；存心要精，不精則受漁；三節要照，四梢要齊；明了三節多一法，明了四梢多一精；起落進退以氣為主，以心為帥；日久思悟，時久運化，朝夕盤打，始而勉強，久而自然。

Chapter 4 Traditional Zhao Bao Tai Chi Theory

6. Methods of Practicing Zhaobao Taichi Kungfu

If you are a beginner in taichi, it is important for you to pay attention to the direction you are facing with each movement you make. Knowing in which direction to move or turn is the foundation of taichi.

If you practice taichi and you are careless or restless, or your mind is not focused, or your eyes do not know where your hands are, or your hand movements are not connected with your foot movements, then you are practicing taichi blindly.

If your whole body is stiff and your hand motions do not lead your feet, then your movements are sudden and furious, and your body movements are ahead of your energy movements. In combat, this results in your opponent being able to see where your energy is going, so he or she can strike you easily. This is called practicing taichi stupidly.

When you practice taichi, your mind and energy movements should be calm, as if nothing is happening. Your eyes should be focused and your spirit should be concentrated. Your body should move lightly, so your shoulders can be relaxed. Your energy should be soft in your movements, so your body can be flexible. Your feet should move naturally, not too fast and not too slow, so your steps can be steady and firm. When your shoulders are relaxed, your body is flexible, and your steps are steady, then your head should be upright and still, so your energy can travel directly from your feet through your shoulders to your hands, to preserve your strength. If your strength moves smoothly, then your energy is united. And if your energy is united, then your strength is powerful.

These are the methods for you to learn when you practice taichi. You should practice them often until you are familiar with them. Then your eyes will be connected with your hand and foot movements, and your mind will be connected with your thought and energy. They all will be united. Then your taichi will be profound and in harmony with nature and truth.

6. 趙堡太極拳練法說明-鄭悟清

夫初練者，宜端正方向以立根基，最忌粗心浮氣精神不屬，眼不顧手、手不顧腳，此謂之盲練也；尤忌身形不活、手腳不隨，即用猛力、處處奪力而反能顯力者，此痴練耳；倘能平心靜氣，注目凝神，輕搖之以松其肩，柔隨之以活其身，徐行之以穩其步；待至肩松、身活、步穩，然後鎮頭領氣，以衛其力，力順則氣自通，氣通則力自重，所學之法如是練而習之，以期純熟，則手、眼、步一致，心、神、氣相同，自能臻自然而然之妙境矣。

7. Tai Chi and Health

Ever since we were born, we've always been in motion. Even during sleep, though still and seemingly inert, our bodies continue to move internally, our hearts pumping, our blood circulating. Our waking and sleeping motions differ only in the magnitude of our movements; our entire lives are the sum process of an infinite number of activities. Every person undergoes the stages of infancy, childhood, adolescence, adulthood, middle age, and old age, and throughout their lifespan, the human body never stops working. Complete stasis happens only at the end of one's life.

Human movement is tied to human well-being, and studies of human well being should take a scientific approach to understanding human wellness. We know, for instance, that excluding our infancy, when we followed our natural instincts, humans have grown to always adapt our movements to the needs of society, such as when we study, work, or complete mundane chores. Take, for example, students who studying in the same posture for hours, or workers who must stay in the same fixed position during work: in these roles we all engage in activities which reduce our muscles natural capabilities and force us to confine our bodies to rigid, unhealthy postures.

Even many of our modern sports exercises can be detrimental to a person's complete health. Many soccer players have repetitive stress injuries to their legs and knees. Tennis players, have similar damage to their wrists, and weight lifters usually experience sever pain in their backs and waists. The more an individual practices a strenuous activity, the more likely they are to experience damage to their bodies. Many professional athletes have so many injuries that they require intensive care even in their

Chapter 4 Traditional Zhao Bao Tai Chi Theory

mid-life stage. Such examples are common and widespread. Human exercise can be divided into two basic categories: activities that burn energy and require a kind of "cost" in the form of energy and muscle power, and activities that are restorative, which reinvigorate and energize. We've already described the types of activities that bring only wear and tear to your body. So how do we engage in exercise that restores and rejuvenates?

Tai Chi is an exemplary form of restorative exercise based on hundreds of years of Chinese practice and experience. Modern medicine has proven that Tai Chi helps prevent age-related heart, cerebral, and blood-related diseases such as coronary heart disease, cerebral hemorrhage, and stroke. People who are engaged in desk jobs that require long periods of sitting—such as software engineers—tend to maintain the same posture for hours. Such habits can restrict blood circulation, cause muscular fatigue along spine, deteriorate vision, and increase blood pressure. Untreated over time, these conditions worsen and become serious hidden injuries. Regular Tai Chi practice purges the toxins that have accumulated in the body, and uses qigong exercises to unify the heart and body into a state of purity.

The movements of Tai Chi are designed to appear soft, natural and fluid and improve the natural grace of the human body. Movements are focused on developing "relaxation, serenity, and fluidity", and based on the principals of "center, balance, and circular movements." These ideals are also supported by hundreds of years of Chinese study and history. Tai Chi exercises seek fluid motion and coordination, and the feet, hands, torso, limbs are trained to move in simultaneously in circular patterns. These motions nurture healthy blood circulation, regular bodily functions. Tai Chi exercises also boost the improve the flow of oxygen throughout the body, and improve immune system, help to one's realize one's true physical and mental potential, and stimulates the human body to its optimal state—goals that follow the saying that, "To come from Nature and return to Nature is the highest form of self-cultivation."

7. 太極拳與養生健身

人的生命自誕生的那一刻起，就沒有停止過運動。包括在睡眠中，人的肢體表面進入休息狀態，但内部器官照常在工作， 例如：心臟照常在跳動，血液依然在流動等等，只是運動的幅度不同而已，實際上人的一生就是運動的過程；真正的停止那就是生命結束的時候。 一個人從出生經過嬰兒期、少年、青年逐漸成人，再邁向中、老年，人的肌體器官及精神意識從沒有停止過工作。

那麼站在養生角度，以科學客觀的標準來評估人一生的動作，除了嬰兒期，嬰兒憑着天賦，遵循大自然的規律做着有利於自身成長發育的動作外，一旦長大進入人為的模式：學習、工作、家務等等勞作，都不是順應生命對肢體的自然要求，而是為了適應人為社會的需要。如學生為了學習長時間所保持的一種姿勢，工人在工作時根據各自行業不同的工作要求，所長達數小時保持的動作姿勢，只是消耗人的體能，對人體本身都不是有益的運動。甚至包括很多現代的體育運動，如足球運動員、其越職業化腿、膝部的傷病越多；網球運動員、越職業其腕部的勞損越重；舉重運動員、成績越好腰部的勞損越大；此類例子涉及面太廣不勝枚舉。

人體的運動本質上有兩種區別：一種是<u>消耗體能</u>，另

Chapter 4 Traditional Zhao Bao Tai Chi Theory

一種是積蓄體能，前面概括了消耗，那麼積蓄體能靠什麼樣的運動呢？

太極拳就是一種優秀而獨特的積蓄體能的運動，它是中華民族歷代先哲們經數百年的不斷醞釀，累積，逐漸形成的。現代醫學也已廣泛證明了太極拳對于預防中、老年心腦血管疾病如冠心病、腦血栓及中風等有明顯的效果。尤其對于久坐人士，如電腦工程師等職業，由于工作性質原因，經常保持一種姿勢長達數小時，造成脊椎疲勞，腦血管僵化，視神經麻痹，視力減退，心臟負荷增加；久而久之，使人體健康潛藏極大隱患；經常參加太極拳練習，能疏通人體全身脈絡，使人體內沉積毒素排出體外，同時通過氣功導引可使人身心合一，完全進入淨化狀態。

太極拳所有的動作姿勢都是針對人體自身肌能的需求而設計的，外表柔和順暢，自然飄逸，內里蘊藏中國傳統文化之精髓，太極拳運動以"中，正，平，圓"為根基，運動起來順其自然，步走圓周，手畫圓周，身行圓周，肢繞圓周，分五行，列八卦，吞六合，斗陰陽，運行氣血，打通全身經脈，修復人體肌能，提高自身免疫力，充分開發人體潛能，回歸人體最佳原始狀態，正所謂：來於自然還於自然，是修身養性的最高境界。

Chapter 5   Zhao Bao Tai Chi Routine
第五章   趙堡太極拳傳統套路

1. The Seventy-Five Movements of Zhaobao Taichi Kungfu
   趙堡太極拳傳統七十五式套路名稱

1. 起式
   Commencing Form
2. 金剛式（含搬攔錘）
   Buddha's Warrior Attendant Pounds Mortar
3. 懶扎衣式
   Lazy about Tying Coat
4. 白鶴亮翅式
   White Crane Spreads Its Wings
5. 單鞭式
   Single Whip
6. 金剛式（含搬攔錘）
   Buddha's Warrior
7. 白鶴亮翅式（側方）
   White Crane Spreads Its Wings
8. 斜形式
   Walking Obliquely
9. 托槍敗勢式（又名叉步躍步）
   Holding the Spear and Staggering

81

Chapter 5 Zhao Bao Tai Chi Routine

10 斜形式

    Walking Obliquely

11 托槍敗勢式（又名叉步躍步）

    Holding the Spear and Staggering

12 躍步金剛式

    Buddha's Warrior Attendant Pounds Mortar

13 懷中抱月式

    Holding the Moon Before the Chest

14 伏虎式（又名打虎拳）

    Hitting the Tiger

15 擒拿串錘式

    Grappling and Continuing to Punch

16 肘底藏錘式

    Fist Under Elbow

17 倒卷肱式

    Step Backward and Whirl Arms

18 白鶴亮翅式（側方）

    White Crane Spreads Its Wings

19 斜形式

    Walking Obliquely

20 閃通背式（含倒掃堂）

    Flashing the Arms

21 白鶴亮翅式

    White Crane Spreads Its Wings

Chapter 5 Zhao Bao Tai Chi Routine

22 單鞭式
Single Whip
23 雲手式
Cloud Hands
24 左高探馬式
High Pat on Horse
25 右插腳式
Setting in Right Foot
26 右高探馬式
High Pat on Horse
27 左插腳式
Setting in Left Foot
28 左卷腳蹬根式
Curve Left Leg and Kick with the Left Heel
29 青龍探海式（又名一步一錘）
Green Dragon Investigates the Sea
30 翻身二起腳式
Flipping-Body Double Foot Raise
31 分門椿抱膝式
Open-Door Pillar Holding Knee
32 鷂子翻身式（又名喜鵲登枝）
Hawk Turns Body
33 右卷腳蹬根式
Curve Right Leg and Kick with the Right Heel

Chapter 5 Zhao Bao Tai Chi Routine

34 分馬掌式

Open-Horse Palm

35 掩手錘式

Hidden Thrust Punch and Whirling Upper Arms

36 左右七寸肘七寸靠式

Left and Right Seven-Inch Elbow and Shoulder

37 抱頭推山式

Embracing Head and Pushing Mountain

38 白鶴亮翅式

White Crane Spreads Its Wings

39 單鞭式

Single Whip

40 前后照式

Forward and Backward Protecting

41 野馬分鬃式

Parting the Wild Horse's Mane

42 玉女穿梭式

Jade Maiden Works Shuttles

43 躍步懶扎衣式

Lazy about Tying Coat

44 白鶴亮翅式

White Crane Spreads Its Wings

45 單鞭式

Single Whip

Chapter 5 Zhao Bao Tai Chi Routine

46 雲手式
Cloud Hands

47 雙風貫耳式（又名童子拜佛）
Strike Opponent's Ears with Both Fists

48 二郎擔山式（又名跌叉掃堂）
Second Lad Carries Mountain

49 左金鷄獨立式
Golden Rooster Stands on Left Leg

50 右金鷄獨立式
Golden Rooster Stands on Right Leg

51 雙跌腳式
Double Drop Leg

52 倒卷肱式
Step Backward and Whirl Arms

53 白鶴亮翅式（側方）
White Crane Spreads Its Wings

54 斜形式
Walking Obliquely

55 閃通背式（含倒掃堂）
Flashing the Arms

56 白鶴亮翅式
White Crane Spreads Its Wings

57 單鞭式
Single Whip

85

Chapter 5 Zhao Bao Tai Chi Routine

58　雲手式
　　Cloud Hands
59　高探馬式
　　High Pat on Horse
60　十字單擺腳式
　　Cross Single-Placing Foot
61　吊打指襠錘式
　　Punch of Hitting Crotch
62　金剛式（含搬攔錘）
　　Buddha's Warrior Attendant Pounds Mortar
63　懶扎衣式
　　Lazy about Tying Coat
64　右扎七星式
　　Right Binding Seven Stars
65　擒拿式
　　Grappling
66　回頭看畫式
　　Turning Head and Looking at Picture
67　白鶴亮翅式
　　White Crane Spreads Its Wings
68　單鞭式
　　Single Whip
69　左扎七星式
　　Left Binding Seven Stars

Chapter 5 Zhao Bao Tai Chi Routine

70 擒拿式

Grappling

71 跨虎式

Straddle the Tiger

72 雙擺腳式

Double Placing Foot

73 挽弓射虎式

Draw the Bow and Shoot the Tiger

74 金剛式（含搬攔錘）

Buddha's Warrior Attendant Pounds Mortar

75 收式（合太極）

Closing Form

2. Illustrations of The Seventy-Five Movements of Zhaobao Taichi Kungfu
趙堡太極拳傳統七十五式套路分解圖

1. Commencing Form

1a. Stand straight with your feet shoulder-width apart, your arms hanging naturally at your sides, and your head upright. Look straight ahead with your mouth closed and your tongue touching the roof of your mouth just in back of your front teeth. Breathe naturally.

1b. Turn your right foot together with your torso 45° to the right, and open both arms like a fan with palms outward.

1c. Step forward with your left foot and lower your body with legs open for a horse stance. At the same time, bring both hands in a half circle up to shoulder level.

1d. Bring your right hand up to the top of your head on the left side, protecting your head. Protect your left temple with your left hand. Bring your right foot forward until it is even with your left foot, and put your weight on your left foot for an empty stance.

1e. Bring both hands gently down to the both side of your body. Stand straight with feet shoulder-width apart.

1 起式

1a 正面站立，雙腳與肩同寬平行，雙手下垂，手背向外，頭部正直，雙目平視，牙齒合攏，舌抵上顎，自然呼吸

1b 右腳與身體同時右轉45度，雙臂呈扇形展開,兩掌心向外

1c 左腿進步，身體下降呈馬步，同時雙手抱圓上升至肩

1d 右手上升護頭，左手護太陽穴，同時右腿跟進虛步

1e 雙手抱球下落自然懸垂，同時右腿還原與肩同寬

Chapter 5 Zhao Bao Tai Chi Routine

1. Commencing Form

1a

1b

1e

1c

1d

2. Buddha's Warrior Attendant Pounds Mortar

2a. Turn your right foot together with your torso 45° to the right. Do not turn your hands.

2b. Bring your left hand forward and your right hand slightly forward as you step forward with your left foot. Lower your body with legs open for a horse stance.

2c. Turn your torso and both hands 45° to the right, preparing to roll back your energy.

2d. Turn your torso and both hands 45° to the left, preparing to press your energy.

2e. Bring your right foot forward until it is even with your left foot, and push your energy down. Move your left hand upward and right hand downward in a circle.

2f. With your weight on your left foot, make a fist with your right hand and turn it upward in a curve. Lower your left hand to your dantian.

2g. Lower your right fist down to your left palm, with your left palm protecting your dantian. Stand straight with feet shoulder-width apart.

2 金剛式
2a 右腳與身體同時右轉45度，雙掌不開
2b 雙掌與左腿同時向前，呈馬步防守姿勢
2c 雙掌與身體同時右轉45度，捋勁待發
2d 雙掌與身體同時回轉45度，擠勁待發
2e 右腿跟步按勁相隨，左手上旋右手下轉
2f 虛步待立，右手上旋握拳左手下轉至丹田
2g 右拳下旋左掌托護于丹田，同時右腿還原與肩同寬

Chapter 5 Zhao Bao Tai Chi Routine

2. Buddha's Warrior Attendant Pounds Mortar

2a

2b

2c

2d

2e

2f

2g

Chapter 5 Zhao Bao Tai Chi Routine

3. Lazy about Tying Coat

3a. Move your right fist up in a curve to the vicinity of your nose, and open your right fist.

3b. Turn both hands 90° in a circular motion, with palms parallel and facing each other.

3c. Continue to turn both hands 90° in a circular motion, bringing your left hand up and right hand down, with palms still facing each other. Take a step with your right foot to the right and shift your weight for a horse stance.

3d. Move your right hand up and outward in a curve to the right (2 o'clock), and lower your left hand to the left side of your crotch, shifting your weight for a right bow stance.

3 懶扎衣式

3a 右拳開掌上升至鼻端

3b 雙手同時右旋90度，兩掌心平行相對

3c 雙手繼續右旋90度，兩掌心上下相對，右腳同時右進一步呈馬步

3d 右手上旋至右前方，左手下降至左腿根部，同時變右弓步

Chapter 5 Zhao Bao Tai Chi Routine

3. Lazy about Tying Coat

3a

3b

3c

3d

4. White Crane Spreads Its Wings

4a. Move your right hand in a curve to the front of your chest, and shift your weight for a left bow stance.

4b. Lower your right hand in front of your body in a curve, and turn your left hand palm up. At the same time, turn your torso to the right.

4c. Bring both hands up in a circle, move your left foot towards your right foot, and put your weight on your right foot for an empty stance.

4d. With thumbs down, your left hand at nose level, your right hand at eyebrow level on the right, and weight on your left foot, stand straight with feet shoulder-width apart.

4 白鶴亮翅

4a 右掌轉至胸前，同時變左弓步

4b 右掌下落引出左掌，身體同時右轉 45 度

4b 雙手抱球上升同時收攏左腿呈虛步

4d 雙掌翻出，左掌至鼻尖前，右掌至右眉梢前，同時左腿還原與肩同寬

4. White Crane Spreads Its Wings

4a

4b

4c

4d

5. Single Whip

5a. Turn both hands left in a curve, with your right hand near the center line of your body.

5b. Turn both hands right in a curve, with your left hand near the center line of your body.

5c. Continue to turn both hands left in a curve. At the same time, step to the left with your left foot, with your right hand near the center line of your body for a left bow stance.

5d. With your left hand on your left (10-11 o'clock), make a half circle with your right hand to the right (1-2 o'clock). At the same time, make a hook with your right hand, and shift your weight. Remain in the left bow stance.

5 單鞭式

5a 雙手向左旋轉，右手居中
5b 雙手向右旋轉，左手居中
5c 雙手繼續向左旋轉，左腳同時左進一步，右手居中呈左弓步
5d 左掌居左前方，右掌劃半圓至左前方同時變勾手呈左弓步

Chapter 5　Zhao Bao Tai Chi Routine

5. Single Whip

5a

5b

5c

5d

6. Buddha's Warrior Attendant Pounds Mortar

Perform #2, but face to the left (10-11 o'clock).

6金剛式 同第 2 式，只是方向轉右 45 度

Chapter 5 Zhao Bao Tai Chi Routine

6 Buddha's Warrior Attendant Pounds Mortar

6a

6b

6c

6d

6e

6f

99

7. White Crane Spreads Its Wings

7a. Bring both hands up in a spiral motion, with your left hand at nose level, and your right hand at eyebrow level on the right.

7b. Lower both hands to the sides of your legs. At the same time, step back with your left foot, and bring your right foot forward until it is even with your left foot.

7c. Bring both hands together and bring them up again in a spiral motion. At the same time, step forward with your right foot in a curve to the right, and step forward with your left foot in a curve to the left.

7d. With your left hand at nose level, and your right hand at eyebrow level on the right, stand straight with feet shoulder-width apart.

7 白鶴亮翅

7a 雙手旋轉上升，左掌至鼻尖前，右掌至右眉梢前
7b 雙掌飄落至兩腿前側，同時左腳后撤一步，右腳相隨
7c 雙手旋轉上升，同時右腳劃弧前進一步，左腳相隨
7d 左掌至鼻尖前，右掌至右眉梢前，雙腿與肩同寬

Chapter 5 Zhao Bao Tai Chi Routine

7. White Crane Spreads Its Wings

7a

7b

7c

7d

8. Walking Obliquely

8a. Lower both hands to the right side of your crotch in a curve, and cross your arms at the wrists. At the same time, turn your torso 45° to the right.

8b. Step back with your left foot for a right bow stance.

8c. Touch your knees with both hands. At the same time, turn your torso 90° to the left for a horse stance.

8d. Move both hands up in a circle to the center of your forehead. Cover your right hand with your left hand, and make a hook with your left hand.

8e. Move your right hand to nose level with a snake-like motion. At the same time, lower your left hand and move it to the bottom of your spine. Shift your weight for a left bow stance.

8 斜形式

8a 雙掌與身體同時右旋，呈十字手面右 45 度

8b 左腿后撤，呈右弓步

8c 雙手分掌摸膝，同時身體左轉 90 度呈馬步

8d 雙手抱球上升交匯于印堂，右掌蓋左勾

8e 右掌蛇行至鼻尖前方，左勾回落身后尾骨處呈左弓步

Chapter 5 Zhao Bao Tai Chi Routine

8. Walking Obliquely

8a

8b

8c

8d

8e

9. Holding the Spear and Staggering

9a. Rotate your right hand until the palm is up. At the same time, move your left hand out as if holding a spear. Move your feet for a left bow stance.

9b. Move your left and right arms 180° to the right. Move your feet for a right bow stance.

9c. Step inward with your right foot. Move your hands as if holding a spear up.

9d. Step back with your left foot for an empty stance. Make a hook with your left hand. Prepare to move as if turning a spear.

9e. Shift your weight to the left foot for an empty stance. Move your hooked left hand up and your right hand down in a curving motion, as if you are picking up an object with a spear.

9 托槍敗勢式

9a 右掌心旋轉翻上，同時出左掌，呈左弓步托槍之勢
9b 左右手翻轉右撤，呈右弓步撤槍之勢
9c 右腿跟進一步，呈順槍之勢
9d 左腿回撤一虛步，左掌變勾，呈翻槍之勢
9e 左腿變實，右腿變虛，左勾翻上，右掌翻下，呈挑槍之勢

Chapter 5 Zhao Bao Tai Chi Routine

9. Holding the Spear and Staggering

9a

9b

9c

9d

9e

10. Stepping and Walking Obliquely

10a. Move both arms in a semicircle, crossing them in the middle of the movement. At the same time, lift your right foot and step over your left knee.

10b. Cross both arms and both feet at the same time, changing your step.

10c-10e. Continue by performing #8c-8e.

10 躍步斜形式
10a　雙臂右旋交叉，同時起右腳躍過左膝
10b　雙臂與雙腿同時交叉換步
10c　10d　10e 同第 8 式

10. Stepping and Walking Obliquely

10a

10b

10c

10d

10e

11. Holding the Spear and Staggering

Perform #9.

11 托槍敗勢式

同第 9 式

Chapter 5 Zhao Bao Tai Chi Routine

11. Holding the Spear and Staggering

11a

11b

11c

11d

11e

12. Buddha's Warrior Attendant Pounds Mortar

12a-12c: Perform 10a-10c in the reverse direction.

12d. Place your right fist on your open left hand in front of your chest. Stand straight with feet shoulder-width apart.

12 躍步金剛式
12a 12b 12c 同第 10 式，只是方向相反

12d 左掌右拳相抱于胸前，雙腿與肩同寬

Chapter 5 Zhao Bao Tai Chi Routine

12. Buddha's Warrior Attendant Pounds

12a

12b

12c

12d

Chapter 5 Zhao Bao Tai Chi Routine

13. Holding the Moon Before the Chest

13a. Open your right fist. At the same time, lower your hands to your dantian.

13b. Cross your arms in front of your chest. Step outward to the right with your right foot for a horse stance.

13 懷中抱月式
13a 右拳開掌同時雙手翻轉下落于丹田
13b 雙臂交叉翻轉合抱于胸前，同時右腳向右一步呈馬步

Chapter 5 Zhao Bao Tai Chi Routine

13. Holding the Moon Before the Chest

13a

13b

Chapter 5 Zhao Bao Tai Chi Routine

14. Hitting the Tiger

14a. Lower your hands to the vicinity of your knees.

14b. Make a fist with your left hand and raise it to your forehead.

14c. Lower your left fist to your waist. At the same time, make a fist with your right hand and raise it to your right temple. Shift your weight for a right bow stance.

14 伏虎式

14a 雙掌內旋下落摸雙膝
14b 左手握拳上升至印堂
14c 左拳自印堂劃圓下落至腰間，同時右手握拳上升至頭右側，呈右弓步

Chapter 5 Zhao Bao Tai Chi Routine

14. Hitting the Tiger

14a

14b 14c

15. Grappling and Continuing to Punch

15a. Lower your right fist with a curving motion. At the same time, open your left fist and raise it with a curving motion, and shift your weight to the left for a left bow stance. Finish by covering your left hand with your right fist in the vicinity of your dantian.

15b. Turn your right fist until the thumb is upward. Move your right fist outward. Make a fist with your left hand. Bring your left foot close to your right foot for an empty stance.

15 擒拿串錘式

15a 右拳劃圓下落，左拳開掌劃圓上升，同時身體向左運行變左弓步，左掌蓋右拳腕交匯于丹田

15b 右拳旋腕擊出，左掌合拳，同時左弓步合攏呈左虛步

Chapter 5 Zhao Bao Tai Chi Routine

15. Grappling and Continuing to Punch

15a

15b

16. Fist Under Elbow

Turn your body to the left. Move your right fist inward and your left fist outward with circular motions. Finish with your left fist protecting your forehead and your right fist under your left elbow.

16 肘底藏錘式
身體左轉，同時雙拳交錯左旋，左拳護面，右拳藏於左肘下

Chapter 5 Zhao Bao Tai Chi Routine

16. Fist Under Elbow

17. Step Backward and Whirl Arms

17a. Open both fists and lower both hands. At the same time, shift your weight to the left for an empty stance.

17b. Move your right arm backward in a semicircle. At the same time, raise your right leg, bending the knee.

17c. Turn your body forward.

17d. Move your right hand down to the vicinity of your dantian to meet your left hand. At the same time, step back with your right foot.

17e. Shift your weight to the back foot. Move your left arm backward in a semicircle. At the same time, raise your left leg, bending the knee.

17f. Move your left hand down to the vicinity of your dantian to meet your right hand. At the same time, step back with your left foot.

17g. Move your left arm backward in a semicircle, and raise your left leg, bending the knee. At the same time turn your body to the right (10-11 o'clock).

17h. Lower both hands to your thigh. Stand straight with feet shoulder-width apart.

17 倒卷肱式

17a 雙拳開掌下落，同時左虛步變右虛步

17b 右手領右腿同時上升劃圓

17c 身體轉至前方

17d 右掌劃圓下蓋于腹前，左掌相合，同時右腿后撤

17e 身體后撤，左手領左腿同時上升劃圓

17f 左掌劃圓下蓋于腹前，右掌相合，同時左腿后撤

17g 左手領左腿同時上升劃圓，同時帶動身體右轉 45 度

17h 手腳同時下落，雙手于腿前側，雙腳與肩同寬

Chapter 5 Zhao Bao Tai Chi Routine

17. Step Backward and Whirl Arms

121

Chapter 5 Zhao Bao Tai Chi Routine

18. White Crane Spreads Its Wings

Perform #7.

白鶴亮翅
同第 7 式

18. White Crane Spreads Its Wings

18a

18b

18c

18d

Chapter 5 Zhao Bao Tai Chi Routine

19. Walking Obliquely
Perform #8.

19 斜形式
同第 8 式

Chapter 5 Zhao Bao Tai Chi Routine

19. Walking Obliquely

19a

19b

19c

19d

19e

125

Chapter 5 Zhao Bao Tai Chi Routine

20. Flashing the Arms

20a. Lower your right hand with a circular motion. Move your left hand to touch your right elbow. At the same time, take a small step inward with your right foot.

20b. Turn your body 45° to the left. Raise your right hand to touch your left elbow. At the same time, take a small step back with your left foot.

20c. Move your right arm around your left arm with a spiral motion, ending in the vicinity of your dantian. Make a hook with your left hand and move it to the bottom of your spine.

20d. Step forward with your left foot. Move your right hand forward. Move your left hand forward.

20e-f. Turn your body 135° to the right, pivoting on your left leg. Swing your arms in the form of an X.

20g. Swing your arms up over your head, protecting your head. Bring your right foot close to your left foot for an empty stance.

20h. Twist your hands to bring the palms outward with thumbs down. With your left hand at nose level, your right hand at eyebrow level on the right, and weight on your left foot, stand straight with feet shoulder-width apart.

20 閃通背式

20a 右手劃圓下落，左手摸右肘上，同時右腳內收一步

20b 身體左轉 45 度，右手抵左肘下，同時左腳回收一步

20c 右掌纏繞下落于丹田，左掌變勾手返回身後尾骨

20d 左腳向前一步，同時出右手，左手相隨

20e-20f 以左腿為軸，身體向右轉 135 度雙手呈 S 形旋轉相隨

20g 以左腿為軸，雙手翻身劃圓護頭，右腿虛步跟隨

20h 雙掌翻出，左掌至鼻尖前，右掌至右眉梢前，同時右腿還原與肩同寬

20. Flashing the Arms

20a

20b

20c

20d

20e

20f

20g

20h

Chapter 5 Zhao Bao Tai Chi Routine

21. White Crane Spreads Its Wings
Perform #7.

白鶴亮翅
21a 雙手向左旋轉，右手居中，同時右腿上前一步
21b 雙手繼續向右旋轉，左手居中，同時左腿跟上一步
21c 雙掌翻出，左掌至鼻尖前，右掌至右眉梢前，同時左腿還原與肩同寬

Chapter 5 Zhao Bao Tai Chi Routine

21. White Crane Spreads Its Wings

21a

21b

21c

Chapter 5 Zhao Bao Tai Chi Routine

22. Single Whip
Perform #5.

22 單鞭式
同前第 5 式

Chapter 5 Zhao Bao Tai Chi Routine

22. Single Whip

22a

22b

22c

22d

Chapter 5 Zhao Bao Tai Chi Routine

23. Cloud Hands

23a. Swing your right arm in a semicircle going up at the center line of your body. At the same time, swing your left arm in a semicircle going down at the center line. Bring your right hand to the vicinity of your dantian.

23b. Swing your left arm in a circle going down at the center line of your body. At the same time, swing your right arm in a semicircle going up at the center line to the top of your head.

23c. Turn your body 90° to the left, and swing your right hand in a circle to your left hand.

23d. Slide your right hand to your left elbow, and shift your weight to your right foot.

23e. Shift your weight to your left foot for a left bow stance. Your left hand protects your chest, and your right hand protects your dantian.

23 雲手式

23a　雙手交替繞環，右手從上至下劃圓至中下方

23b　左手從上至下劃圓至中下方，右手從下至上劃圓至右上方

23c　身體左轉 90 度，右手劃圓至左手梢

23d　右手從左手梢滑落至肘，左腿呈虛步

23e　左腿落實呈左弓步，左手護胸，右手護腹

Chapter 5 Zhao Bao Tai Chi Routine

23. Cloud Hands

133

Chapter 5 Zhao Bao Tai Chi Routine

24. High Pat on Horse
With both hands as if they are holding a ball, swing both hands up and to the left. At the same time, raise your left leg and move it to the right

24 左高探馬式
雙手抱球向左旋轉，同時左腳向右翻起

24. High Pat on Horse

25. Setting in Right Foot

25a. Lower your left foot to the ground. At the same time, step forward with your right foot for a right bow stance. Your right hand protects your chest, and your left hand protects your dantian.

25b. Make fists with both hands. Move them to protect your upper front body.

25c. Move both fists down as if your are breaking an object. At the same time, lower your body as if you are sitting.

25d. Move both fists up in a spiral motion. At the same time, raise your body. Move your right foot back inward for an empty stance.

25e. Open both fists. At the same time, raise your right leg.

25f. Cover the top with both hands and strike out with both hands. Kick your right hand with your right foot.

25 右插腳式
25a 左腳落地同時進右腿呈右弓步，右手護胸左手護腹
25b 雙掌變拳防守于面前
25c 雙拳下砸，身體同時下沉
25d 雙拳繞環上升，身體起立同時收右腳呈虛步
25e 雙拳開掌同時起右腿
25f 雙掌蓋頂擊出，右腳踢擊右掌

Chapter 5 Zhao Bao Tai Chi Routine

25. Setting in Right Foot

25a

25b

25c

25d

25e

25f

26. High Pat on Horse
Perform #24 in the reverse direction.

26 右高探馬式
雙手抱球向右旋轉，同時右腳下落向左翻起

Chapter 5 Zhao Bao Tai Chi Routine

26. High Pat on Horse

27. Setting in Left Foot
Perform #25 in the reverse direction.

27 左插脚式 同第 25 式，只是方向相反

Chapter 5 Zhao Bao Tai Chi Routine

27. Setting in Left Foot

27a

27b

27c

27d

27e

27f

28. Curve Left Leg and Kick with Left Heel

28a. Lower both hands to the sides of your body. At the same time, lower your left foot to your right knee.

28b. Make fists with both hands. Bring your fists together between your chest and your dantian. At the same time, turn your body 90° to the left. Raise your left knee.

28c. Turn both fists to the back and open both arms. At the same time, kick your left heel to the left side of your body.

28 左卷腳蹬根式
28a 雙掌下落至身側，左腳同時下落至右膝
28b 雙掌握拳合攏于胸腹之間，同時身體左轉 90 度左腿提膝
28c 雙拳向后旋轉舒展雙臂，同時左腿用腳跟向身體左側蹬出

Chapter 5 Zhao Bao Tai Chi Routine

28. Curve Left Leg and Kick with Left Heel

28a

28b

28c

Chapter 5 Zhao Bao Tai Chi Routine

29. Green Dragon Investigates the Sea

29a. Lower your left foot to the ground. At the same time, strike your left toes with your right fist.

29b. Step with your right foot, and strike your right toes with your left hand.

29c. With your left foot, take a big step forward for a left bow stance. At the same time, strike the right side of your left knee with your right fist with a circular motion.

29 青龍探海式
29a 左腳落地，同時右拳砸于左腳尖上方
29b 右腳上步，同時左拳砸于右腳尖上方
29c 左腳向前跨一大步呈左弓步，同時右拳掄圓砸向左膝右前方

Chapter 5 Zhao Bao Tai Chi Routine

29. Green Dragon Investigates the Sea

29a

29b

29c

145

30. Flipping-Body Double Foot Raise

30a. Protect your head with your right fist. Protect your face with your left fist.

30b. Turn your body 180° to the right, leading with both fists. Keep your body straight and turn both fists outward.

30c. Turn both fists and, with both fists leading, lower your body. Jump. Raise your right knee and, opening both fists

30d. kick both hands with the top of your right foot.

30 翻身二起腳式
30a 右拳護頭，左拳護臉
30b 雙拳帶領身體向身后右轉 180 度，身體立直雙拳翻出
30c 雙拳繞環帶領身體下沉后騰空而起，提左膝踢右腳
30d 雙拳同時開掌拍擊右腳背

Chapter 5 Zhao Bao Tai Chi Routine

30. Flipping-Body Double Foot Raise

30a

30b

30d

30c

147

31. Open-Door Pillar Holding Knee

31a. Lower both feet to the ground for a right horse stand. Cross both hands in front of your body, with your left hand on top, with a motion like two knives.

31b. Raise your body. Move your left foot inward for an empty stance. Turn both hands in front of your body with your palms out.

31c. Turn both hands outward with a circular motion and, with both hands leading, lower your body. Grasp your left knee with both hands, one on each side of your knee.

31d. Raise your left knee with one hand on each side. At the same time, straighten your body.

31 分門樁抱膝式

31a 雙腳落地后呈馬步右側式，雙掌插出左上右下交叉于身前，立掌如雙刀

31b 起身收左腳呈虛步，雙掌外翻于面前，掌心向外

31c 雙掌向外繞圓帶領身體同時下沉，雙掌抱于左膝兩側

31d 雙掌抱左膝上提，同時身體起立

31. Open-Door Pillar Holding Knee

31a

31b

31c

31d

32. Hawk Turns Body

32a. Hold your left knee to your chest with both hands.

32b. Turn your hands until your palms are up and your thumbs out. Kick out with your left heel.

32c. Lower your left foot and sweep outward and backward with your left foot. At the same time, lower both hands to the sides of your body.

32d. Raise your right hand to protect your face.

32e. Raise your left arm to protect your head. At the same time, turn your body to the right, twisting to the right your torso, your left hip, and your left leg.

32f. Protect your head with your left hand. Protect your face with your right hand. Turn your body 270° to the right, twisting to the right your torso, your left hip, and your left leg.

32g. Stand still. Lower both hands naturally to the sides of your body.

32 鷂子翻身式

32a 雙掌提膝于胸前
32b 雙掌外翻，同時左腿以腳跟正面蹬出
32c 左腳下落回勾，雙掌同時下落于身側
32d 起右手護臉
32e 左手向上繞環護頭，同時身體右轉帶動左腿旋跨
32f 左手護頭，右手護臉，身體帶動左腿旋跨右轉 270 度
32g 落地生根，雙掌自然懸垂于身側

Chapter 5 Zhao Bao Tai Chi Routine

32. Hawk Turns Body

32a

32b

32c

32e

32f

32d

32g

151

33. Curve Right Leg and Kick with Right Heel

33a. Raise your right hand. At the same time, raise your right leg with a spiral motion, moving your right leg outward and forward.

33b. Raise your right hand in front of your chest. Raise your right knee to the front of your dantian.

33c. Turn your right palm outward. At the same time, kick your right heel to the right side of your body.

33 右卷腳蹬根式
33a 右手帶動右腿自外而內繞環上提
33b 右手立掌于胸前，右腿提膝于腹前
33c 右掌側外翻出，帶動右腿同時以腳跟向右側蹬出

Chapter 5 Zhao Bao Tai Chi Routine

33. Curve Right Leg and Kick with Right Heel

33a

33b

33c

153

34. Open-Horse Palm

34a. Lower your right foot. At the same time, strike the right side of your right leg with your right hand.

34b. Turn your body 90° to the right. At the same time, strike the left side of your left leg with your left hand.

34c. Lower both hands naturally to the sides of your body.

34 分馬掌式
34a 右腳落地，同時右掌拍擊右腿側
34b 身體右轉 90 度，同時左掌拍擊左腿側
34c 雙掌自然懸垂于身側

Chapter 5 Zhao Bao Tai Chi Routine

34. Open-Horse Palm

34a

34b

34c

35. Hidden Thrust Punch and Whirling Upper Arms

35a. Swing both hands upward and from left to right to protect the left side of your body.

35b. As you continue to swing both hands from left to right, turn your body 90º to the right to protect the right side of your body.

35c. Swing both hands from the upper right to the lower left, and turn your body 135º to the left. At the same time, take a big step to the left with your left foot for a left bow stance. Make a fist with your right hand, cover it with your left hand, and strike with your right fist.

35 掩手錘式
35a 雙掌自左而右繞圓上升，保護左側
35b 雙掌繼續帶動身體繞圓轉右 90 度，保護右側
35c 雙掌自上而下繼續帶動身體繞圓轉左 135 度，同時左腿向左邁一大步呈左弓步，左手掌掩右手錘擊出

Chapter 5 Zhao Bao Tai Chi Routine

35. Hidden Thrust Punch and Whirling Upper Arms

35a

35b

35c

36. Left and Right Seven-Inch Elbow and Shoulder

36a. Open your right fist. Lower both hands to your left knee with a knife-like motion. Lower your left elbow until it is seven inches above the ground.

36b. Make a fist with your right hand and protect your head with it. Protect your face with your left hand. At the same time, straighten your body.

36c. Protect your head with your left hand. Protect your face with your right fist. At the same time, turn your body 180° to the right.

36d. Lower your left hand. Lower your right fist to the front of your right knee. Lower your right elbow until it is seven inches above the ground.

36 左右七寸肘七寸靠式

36a 右拳開掌，雙掌如刀于左膝前劈開，左肘下落至地面七寸處

36b 右掌握拳護頭，左掌護臉，同時挺身

36c 左掌護頭，右拳護臉，同時身體向右旋轉 180 度

36d 左掌劈右拳落于右膝前，右肘下落至地面七寸處

Chapter 5 Zhao Bao Tai Chi Routine

36. Left and Right Seven-Inch Elbow and Shoulder

36b

36c

36d

159

37. Embracing Head and Pushing Mountain

37a. Open your right fist. Raise both hands at the sides of your body with a circular motion to protect both sides of your head.

37b. Use your energy to push your strength out from your chest.

37 抱頭推山式
37a 右拳開掌，雙手抱圓上升保護頭部兩側
37b 以氣催力當胸推出

37. Embracing Head and Pushing Mountain

Chapter 5 Zhao Bao Tai Chi Routine

38. White Crane Spreads Its Wings
Perform #4.

38 白鹤亮翅式
同前第4式

Chapter 5 Zhao Bao Tai Chi Routine

38. White Crane Spreads Its Wings

38a

38b

38c

Chapter 5 Zhao Bao Tai Chi Routine

39. Single Whip
Perform #5.

39 單鞭式
同前第 5 式

Chapter 5 Zhao Bao Tai Chi Routine

9. Single Whip

39a

39b

39c

39d

Chapter 5 Zhao Bao Tai Chi Routine

40. Forward and Backward Protecting

40a. Open your right hand. Move your right hand to the front of your chest with a circular motion.

40b. Move your left hand under your right hand in front of your dantian. Your hands are touching, with the back of your left hand up and the palm of your right hand up. At the same time, turn your body to the right for a right bow stance.

40 前后照式

40a 右勾手開掌劃弧綫于身前正中

40b 左掌合于右掌下，雙掌交匯于腹前正中，手背相貼，同時身體向右運行變右弓步

40. Forward and Backward Protecting

40a

40b

Chapter 5 Zhao Bao Tai Chi Routine

41. Parting the Wild Horse's Mane

41a. Turn your body 90° to the right. At the same time, Separate your hands like two knives. Protect your chest with your right hand, and protect your dantian with your left hand.

41b. Lower your right hand with a circular motion. At the same time, move your right foot inward for an empty stance.

41c. Move your right hand upward with a spiral motion, and step forward with your right foot. Protect your face with your right hand, and protect your dantian with your left hand.

41d. Lower your right hand with a circular motion. Move your left hand upward with a spiral motion, and step forward with your left foot. Protect your face with your left hand, and protect your dantian with your right hand.

41e. Lower your left hand with a circular motion. Move your right hand upward with a spiral motion, and step forward with your right foot. Protect your face with your right hand, and protect your dantian with your left hand.

41 野馬分鬃式

41a 身體右轉 90 度，同時分掌如刀，右手護胸，左手護腹

41b 右掌劃圓下落，同時帶動右腿回收，呈右虛步

41c 右掌繞環上升帶動右步前進，右手護臉，左手護腹

41d 右掌劃圓下落，左掌繞環上升帶動左步前進，左手護臉，右手護腹

41e 左掌劃圓下落，右掌繞環上升帶動右步前進，右手護臉，左手護腹

Chapter 5 Zhao Bao Tai Chi Routine

41. Parting the Wild Horse's Mane

41a

41b

41c

41d

41e

169

42. Jade Maiden Works Shuttles

42a. Move both hands to the right with a circular motion. At the same time, swing your right foot up and to the left.

42b. Bring both hands together. Move your left hand to your right elbow. Kick your opponent's knee with your right foot.

42c. Lower your right foot and turn your body 90° to the right pivoting on your right leg.

42d. As your turn your body to the right, strike with your left elbow, and touch your left elbow with your right hand. Stand with your feet shoulder-width apart.

42 玉女穿梭式

42a 雙手繞圓往右旋轉，同時右腳向左翻起

42b 雙手內合，左手轉至右肘彎，同時右腳鏟擊膝部位置

42c 右腳落地為軸，身體右轉 90 度，

42d 左肘隨身體右轉同時擊出，左肘接觸右手掌，兩腿與肩同寬

Chapter 5 Zhao Bao Tai Chi Routine

42. Jade Maiden Works Shuttles

42a

42b

42c

42d

171

43. Stepping and Lazy about Tying Coat

43a. Rotate your right arm under and around your left arm, and raise your right arm from your elbow. At the same time, turn your body 180° to the right.

43b. Complete the leg movement with a right bow and left arrow stance. Move your right hand up and to the right with a spiral motion. Move your left hand down to the Left side of your crotch.

43 躍步懶扎衣式

43a 右手掌纏繞左手臂由內而外向上盤旋，同時帶動身體右轉 180 度

43b 定勢為右弓左箭步，右手上旋至右前方，左手下降至左腿根部

43. Stepping and Lazy about Tying Coat

43a

43b

Chapter 5 Zhao Bao Tai Chi Routine

44. White Crane Spreads Its Wings

Perform #4.

44 白鹤亮翅式
同前第4式

44. White Crane Spreads Its Wings

44a

44b

44c

44d

Chapter 5 Zhao Bao Tai Chi Routine

45. Single Whip
Perform #5.

45 單鞭式
同前第 5 式

45. Single Whip

45a

45b

45c

45d

46. Cloud Hands

46a-b. Perform #23a-b.

46c. Swing your left arm in a circle going down at the center line of your body. At the same time, step inward with your left leg.

46d. Swing your right arm in a circle going down at the center line of your body. At the same time, step inward with your right leg.

46e. Lower both hands to the sides of your body, with your feet shoulder-width apart.

46 雲手式

46a - 46b 同前第 23 a - 23b 式

46c 左手劃圓帶動左腿內收一步

46d 右手劃圓帶動右腿內收一步

46e 雙掌自然懸垂于身側，雙腳與肩同寬

Chapter 5 Zhao Bao Tai Chi Routine

46. Cloud Hands

46a

46b

46c

46d

46e

Chapter 5 Zhao Bao Tai Chi Routine

47. Strike Opponent's Ears with Both Fists

47a. Raise both hands to the level of your upper lip.

47b. Continue to raise both hands to forehead level, and separate them.

47c. Let both hands fall to the sides of your body.

47d. Make fists with both hands, and strike by bringing them towards each other in front of your body. At the same time, raise your right knee and strike energetically with it.

47 雙風貫耳式
47a 雙手自丹田交合上升至人中穴
47b 雙手繼續上升至印堂穴后分開
47c 雙手自然飄落于身兩側
47d 雙掌握拳合擊于身前，同時提右膝相撞，以氣催力

Chapter 5 Zhao Bao Tai Chi Routine

47. Strike Opponent's Ears with Both Fists

47a

47b

47c

47d

48. Second Lad Carries Mountain

48a. Stamp with your right foot, making a sound with it. At the same time, open both fists, and bring both hands to your chest.

48b. As you stamp with your right foot, move your left foot outward. Open your arms.

48c. Lower your hands with a wood-chopping motion. At the same time, lower your body. Straighten your left leg with your heel on the ground and your toes up, and bend your right knee.

48d. Inhale and expand your chest. Lower the toes of your left foot to the ground for a bow stance. Bring both hands together into a knife-like position.

48e. Turn your body 180° to the left. Protect your chest with your left hand, and strike your opponent's waist with your right hand with a wood-chopping motion. At the same time, sweep your right leg outward and to the right to trip your opponent.

48f. Raise both hands over your head, bring both hands back, and lower both hands to your ears.

48g. Lower both hands in front of your chest, and continue lowering both hands to your legs. At the same time, lower your body, and bend both knees slightly for a half-horse stance.

48 二郎擔山式

48a 右腳跺地震氣有聲，同時雙拳開掌交匯于胸前

48b 右腳跺地的同一瞬間，即出左腳，同時雙臂劃圓舒展

48c 雙掌如刀向兩側劈下，同時全身下沉，左腿直右腿曲呈左跌叉之勢

48d 提氣上升，左腿曲起呈弓步，雙手收掌架刀

48e 身體左轉180度，左掌護胸，右掌如刀攔腰旋劈至腹部，同時右腿掃堂

48f 雙手同時上升過頭至耳后

48g 雙掌同時順前胸按下至腿部，同時帶動全身下沉，微曲雙腿呈半馬步

Chapter 5 Zhao Bao Tai Chi Routine

48. Second Lad Carries Mountain

48a

48b

48c

48d

48e

48f

48g

183

49. Golden Rooster Stands on Left Leg

49a. Raise your right hand over your head, raising your right leg, and bending your right knee. At the same time, raise your body, making a hook with your left hand.

49b. Lower your right hand to your chest, keeping your right hand upright. Lower your body slightly without changing your posture.

49c. Raise your right hand with a spiral motion, raise your right knee slightly, and turn your body 90° to the right.

49 左金鷄獨立式

49a 右手引領右腿上升呈左金鷄獨立之勢，同時帶動全身提起，右手過頭，左手提勾

49b 右手立掌如刀降至胸前，全身微沉保持左金鷄獨立之勢

49c 右手上旋，微提右膝帶動身體右轉 90 度

Chapter 5 Zhao Bao Tai Chi Routine

49. Golden Rooster Stands on Left Leg

50. Golden Rooster Stands on Right Leg

50a. Lower your right hand, and lower your right leg to the ground. At the same time, raise your left hand, and move your left hand over your head as if you are brushing your hair over your ear and downward.

50b. Lower both hands to your legs. At the same time, lower your body, and bend both knees slightly for a half-horse stance.

50c. Raise your left hand over your head, raising your left leg, and bending your left knee. At the same time, raise your body. Lower your right hand to the right side of your body.

50 右金雞獨立式

50a 右手領右腿下降落地，同時左手上升呈梳妝之勢過頭自耳後緩緩下降

50b 雙手下降至腿同時帶動全身下沉，微曲雙腿呈半馬步

50c 左手引領左腿上升呈右金雞獨立之勢，同時帶動全身提起，左手過頭，右手按掌于身側

Chapter 5 Zhao Bao Tai Chi Routine

50. Golden Rooster Stands on Right Leg

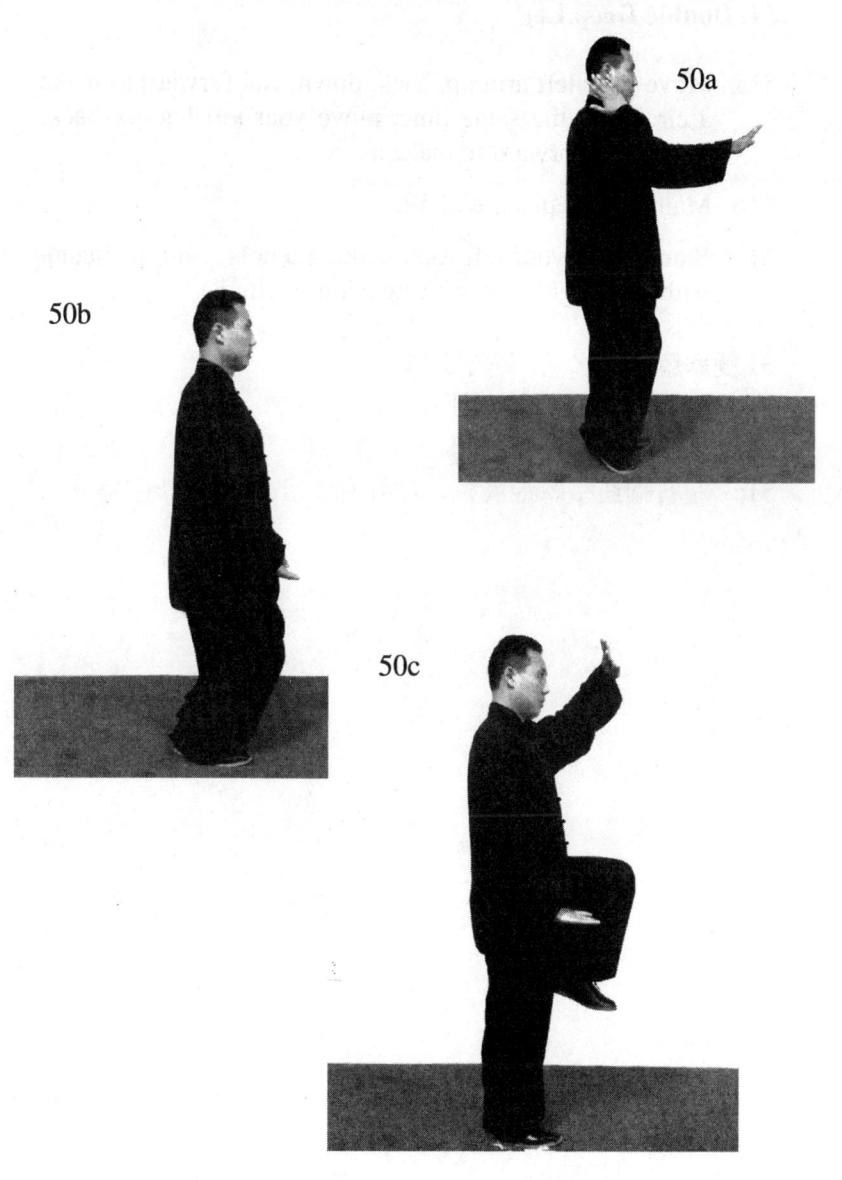

50a

50b

50c

51. Double Drop Leg

51a. Move your left arm up, back, down, and forward to make a circle. At the same time, move your left leg up, back, down, and forward to make a circle.

51b. Maintain the posture of 50c.

51c. Stamp with your left foot, making a noise with it. Stamp with your right foot, making a noise with it.

51 雙跌腳式

51a 左手領左腿繞環一圈

51b 保持右金鷄獨立之勢

51c 左右腳連續跺地震氣，發聲有二

Chapter 5 Zhao Bao Tai Chi Routine

51. Double Drop Leg

51a

51b

51c

Chapter 5 Zhao Bao Tai Chi Routine

52. Step Backward and Whirl Arms
Perform #17.

52 倒卷肱式
同前第 17 式

Chapter 5 Zhao Bao Tai Chi Routine

52. Step Backward and Whirl Arms

53. White Crane Spreads Its Wings
Perform #18.

53 白鹤亮翅式
同前第 18 式

Chapter 5 Zhao Bao Tai Chi Routine

53. White Crane Spreads Its Wings

53a

53b

53c

53d

Chapter 5 Zhao Bao Tai Chi Routine

54. Walking Obliquely
Perform #19.

54 斜形式
同前第 19 式

Chapter 5 Zhao Bao Tai Chi Routine

54. Walking Obliquely

54a

54b

54c

54d

54e

Chapter 5 Zhao Bao Tai Chi Routine

55. Flashing the Arms
Perform #20.

55 闪通背式
同前第 20 式

Chapter 5 Zhao Bao Tai Chi Routine

55. Flashing the Arms

55a

55b

55c

55f

55e

55d

55g

55h

Chapter 5 Zhao Bao Tai Chi Routine

56. White Crane Spreads Its Wings
Perform #21.

56 白鹤亮翅式
同前第 21 式

Chapter 5 Zhao Bao Tai Chi Routine

56. White Crane Spreads Its Wings

56a

56b

56c

Chapter 5 Zhao Bao Tai Chi Routine

57. Single Whip
Perform #22.

57 單鞭式
同前第 22 式

Chapter 5 Zhao Bao Tai Chi Routine

57. Single Whip

57a

57b

57c

57d

58. Cloud Hands

58a-b. Perform 23a-23b

58c. Lower your right hand to the right side of your body with a circular motion. At the same time, move your right foot inward. Raise your left hand with a circular motion over the left side of your head.

58d. Raise your right hand with a circular motion over the right side of your head. At the same time, move your right foot forward in a half step, and then move your right foot to the right in a half step. Lower your left hand to the left side of your body with a circular motion.

58 雲手式

58a－58b 同前第 23a －23b 式

58c 右手劃圓下落至身右側，同時帶動右腿內收一步，左手劃圓上升至頭左側

58d 右手繼續劃圓上升至頭右側，同時右腳繞弧綫上前半步，左手劃圓下落至身 左側

58. Cloud Hands

58a

58b

58c

58d

59. High Pat on Horse

59a. Rotate your arms around each other in a circle, ending with your right hand over your left hand.

59b. Lower your right hand to protect your dantian, and protect your chest with your left hand. At the same time, move your left foot outward for a left bow stance.

59c. Move your left foot back for an empty stance. At the same time, rotate your hands counterclockwise 180° as if you are holding a ball.

59 高探馬式
59a 雙手盤旋，右手繞過左手梢
59b 左手領左腳上前一步呈左弓步，左手護胸，右手護腹
59c 撤左腳內旋，雙手抱球左旋 180 度，呈左前虛步

Chapter 5 Zhao Bao Tai Chi Routine

59. High Pat on Horse

59a

59b

59c

Chapter 5 Zhao Bao Tai Chi Routine

60. Cross Single-Placing Foot

60a. Move your left foot forward for a left bow stance. At the same time, rotate your hands clockwise 180° as if you are holding a ball. Bring both arms in front of your body. Your left hand protects the front of your body, and your right hand is under your left armpit.

60b. Raise your right foot, and kick with your right foot forward and to the left.

60c. Move your right foot outward with a circular motion, and move your right foot to the back of your body.

60d. Kick your left hand with your right foot, making a noise with it. Lower your right foot to the back of your body.

60 十字單擺腳式

60a 左腳上前一步呈左弓步，同時雙手抱球右旋180度，兩臂交合，左掌 護于身前，右掌架于左腋下
60b 起右腳踢向左前上方
60c 右腳從左前上方劃弧綫掃向右后方
60d 右腳從左前上方劃弧綫踢中左手掌響亮發聲，向右后方飄落

Chapter 5 Zhao Bao Tai Chi Routine

60. Cross Single-Placing Foot

60a

60b

60c

60d

61. Punch of Hitting Crotch

Lower your right foot to the ground. Make a fist with your left hand. Move your left fist to the left side of your waist with a small clockwise circular motion. At the same time, make a fist with your right hand. Move your right fist to the right side of your crotch with a big counterclockwise circular motion.

61 吊打指襠錘式
右腳落地生根，左掌握拳繞小圈至腰部，右掌握拳順勢繞大圈吊打至襠部

61. Punch of Hitting Crotch

Chapter 5 Zhao Bao Tai Chi Routine

62. Buddha's Warrior Attendant Pounds Mortar
Perform #2.

62 金刚式
同前第 2 式

Chapter 5 Zhao Bao Tai Chi Routine

62. Buddha's Warrior Attendant Pounds Mortar

211

Chapter 5 Zhao Bao Tai Chi Routine

63. Lazy about Tying Coat
Perform #3.

63 懒扎衣式
同前第 3 式

Chapter 5 Zhao Bao Tai Chi Routine

63. Lazy about Tying

63a

63b

63c

63d

64. Right Binding Seven Stars

64a. Raise your left hand, and make a half circle upward and to the right with both hands. Keep your weight on your right foot for a right bow stance.

64b. Continue to make a half circle downward and to the left with both hands. Shift your weight to your left foot for a left bow stance.

64c. Turn your torso to the right. Hold both hands up like two knives.

64d. Protect your left ear with your left hand. Lower your right hand with a wood-chopping motion. At the same time, Lower your body. Straighten your right leg with your heel on the ground and your toes up, and bend your left knee.

64 右扎七星式

64a 起左手雙掌向右旋轉，呈右弓步防守姿勢
64b 雙掌繼續由下往上向左旋轉，呈左弓步防守姿勢
64c 襠胯右旋，雙手立掌如刀
64d 左掌護左耳，右掌順勢劈下，同時帶動全身下沉，右腿直左腿曲呈右跌叉之勢

64. Right Binding Seven Stars

64a

64b

64c

64d

65. Grappling

65a. Inhale. Raise your energy. Bend your right knee for a bow stance. Hold your right hand up like a knife. Touch your right elbow with your left hand.

65b. Move your arms in circles around each other in front of your chest. At the same time, shift your weight for a horse stance.

65c. Make fists with both hands and grapple. Lower your energy to your dantian.

65 擒拿式
65a 提氣上升，右腿曲起呈弓步，右掌架刀，左手摸右肘
65b 雙臂纏繞至胸前，同時右弓步變馬步
65c 雙掌擒拿握拳氣沉丹田

Chapter 5 Zhao Bao Tai Chi Routine

65. Grappling

65a

65b

65c

Chapter 5 Zhao Bao Tai Chi Routine

66. Turning Head and Looking at Picture

66a. Strike with your left fist to the right (1 o'clock) with a hooking motion. At the same time, turn your torso to the right and raise your left knee.

66b. Move your left knee to the right and then to the left with a sweeping motion, and kick with your left foot.

66c. Lower your left foot to the ground. Pivoting on your left leg, turn your right leg to the left with a circular motion, and step forward with your right foot. Protect your face with your left fist, and strike your opponent's crotch with your right fist.

66d. Lower both elbows and protect your face with both fists. Lower your dantian for a horse stance.

66 回頭看畫式

66a 左勾拳向右上方擊出，同時右旋腰胯帶動左膝提起
66b 左膝向右上提后旋左外擺掃踢
66c 左腳落地后為軸，右腿旋左上步、左拳護面，右拳擊襠
66d 后沉雙肘，雙拳護面，馬步沉襠

Chapter 5 Zhao Bao Tai Chi Routine

66. Turning Head and Looking at Picture

66a

66b

66c

66d

67. White Crane Spreads Its Wings
Perform #21 in the reverse direction.

67 白鹤亮翅式
同前第 21 式，只是方向相反

Chapter 5 Zhao Bao Tai Chi Routine

67. White Crane Spreads Its Wings

67a

67b

67d

67c

68. Single Whip
Perform #22 in the reverse direction.

68 單鞭式
同前第 22 式，只是方向相反

Chapter 5 Zhao Bao Tai Chi Routine

68. Single Whip

68a

68b

68c

68d

69. Left Binding Seven Stars
Perform #64 in the reverse direction.

69 左扎七星式
同前第 64 式，只是方向相反

Chapter 5 Zhao Bao Tai Chi Routine

69. Left Binding Seven Stars

69a

69b

69c

69d

225

70. Grappling
Perform #65 in the reverse direction.

70 擒拿式
同前第65式，只是方向相反

Chapter 5 Zhao Bao Tai Chi Routine

70. Grappling

70a

70b

70c

71. Straddle the Tiger

71a. Cross your hands in front of your chest. At the same time, step inward with your right foot.

71b. Open both fists and lower both hands. At the same time, lower your body as if you are sitting for a horse stance. touch your knees with both hands.

71c. Bring both hands up to your forehead as if they are holding a ball. Make a hook with your left hand, and cover your hooked left hand with your right hand. At the same time, step inward with your left foot for an empty stance.

71d. Lower your right arm, ending in the vicinity of your dantian. Move your hooked left hand to the bottom of your spine.

71e. Raise your right hand and turn your body to the right.

71f. Raise your left hand. At the same time, raise your left knee.

71g. Turn both hands 180° to the right. At the same time, turn your left leg and your body.

71 跨虎式

71a 雙拳合十于胸前，同時右腳內收一步

71b 雙拳開掌下落，同時帶動身體下沉呈馬步，雙手摸于兩膝外側

71c 雙手抱球上升至印堂，右掌蓋左勾，同時左腳內收一步呈左虛步

71d 右掌下落於丹田，左勾手回歸身後尾骨

71e 起右掌帶動身體右轉

71f 左掌帶動左腿提膝相隨

71g 雙掌帶動左腿旋跨，同時全身轉右180度

Chapter 5 Zhao Bao Tai Chi Routine

71. Straddle the Tiger

71a

71b

71c

71d

71e

71f

71g

Chapter 5 Zhao Bao Tai Chi Routine

72. Double Placing Foot

72a. Lower your left foot and pivot on your left leg. Protect your upper front body with both hands.

72b. Raise your right foot, and kick forward and to the left with your right foot.

72c. Move your right foot outward with a circular motion, and move your right foot to the back of your body.

72d. Kick both hands high up with your right foot, moving your right foot from left to right and making two noises with it. Lower your right foot to the back of your body.

72 雙擺腳式

72a 左腳落地為軸，雙掌防守于身前
72b 起右腳踢向左前上方
72c 右腳從左前上方劃弧綫掃向右后方
72d 右腳從左前上方劃弧綫踢中左右雙掌，發出兩聲響亮聲音向右后方飄落

Chapter 5 Zhao Bao Tai Chi Routine

72. Double Placing Foot

72a

72b

72c

72d

Chapter 5 Zhao Bao Tai Chi Routine

73. Draw the Bow and Shoot the Tiger

73a. Lower your right foot to the ground. Lower both hands and make fists with them. At the same time, move your fists along your sides to the back of your body with a circular motion.

73b. Move your fists to the front of your body with a circular motion, ending as if you are drawing a bow to shoot a tiger.

73 挽弓射虎式

73a 右腳落地生根，雙掌順勢落下，同時握拳向身後繞圓

73b 雙拳繞圓轉回身前，呈挽弓射虎之勢

73. Draw the Bow and Shoot the Tiger

73a

73b

74. Buddha's Warrior Attendant Pounds Mortar
Perform #2.

74 金剛式
同前第2式

Chapter 5 Zhao Bao Tai Chi Routine

74. Buddha's Warrior Attendant Pounds Mortar

75. Closing Form

75a. Turn your body 45° to the right. At the same time, open your fists and step back with your right foot.

75b. Turn your body 45° to the left. At the same time, raise both hands to shoulder level with a semicircular motion.

75c. Raise your right hand to the top of your head on the left side, protecting your head. Protect your left temple with your left hand. At the same time, move your left foot inward for an empty stance.

75d. Bring both hands down gently as if you are holding a ball, and move them to the sides of your body. Stand straight with feet shoulder-width apart.

75 收式（合太極）

75a 身體右轉 45 度，同時開雙掌，右腿后撤一步

75b 身體向左回轉 45 度，同時雙掌抱圓上升至肩

75c 右手上升護頭，左手護太陽穴，同時左腿回撤呈虛步

75d 雙手抱球下落自然懸垂，同時右腿還原與肩同寬

Chapter 5 Zhao Bao Tai Chi Routine

75. Closing Form

75a

75b

75c

75d

Chapter 6
Zhao Bao Tai Chi Kung Fu
第六章
趙堡太極拳技擊功夫

1. Zhao Bao Tai Chi Push Hands
趙堡太極推手跌法

Henry Carrabello, Master Peng, Wei Jim Lai

Chapter 6 Zhao Bao Tai Chi Kung Fu

Zhao Bao Tai Chi Push Hands

1 左捋槍杆

Chapter 6 Zhao Bao Tai Chi Kung Fu

Zhao Bao Tai Chi Push Hands

2 倒卷肱

Chapter 6 Zhao Bao Tai Chi Kung Fu

Zhao Bao Tai Chi Push Hands

3 高探馬

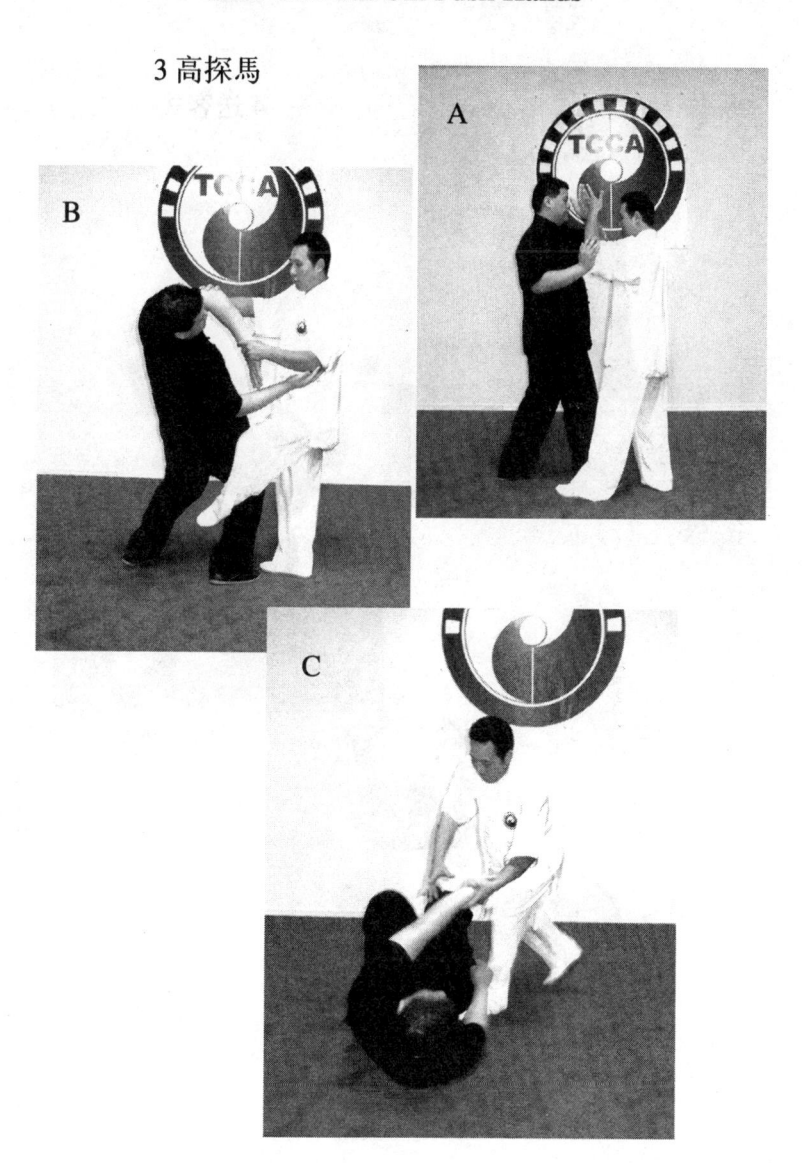

Chapter 6 Zhao Bao Tai Chi Kung Fu

Zhao Bao Tai Chi Push Hands

4 送客式

Chapter 6 Zhao Bao Tai Chi Kung Fu

Zhao Bao Tai Chi Push Hands

5 外捌手

243

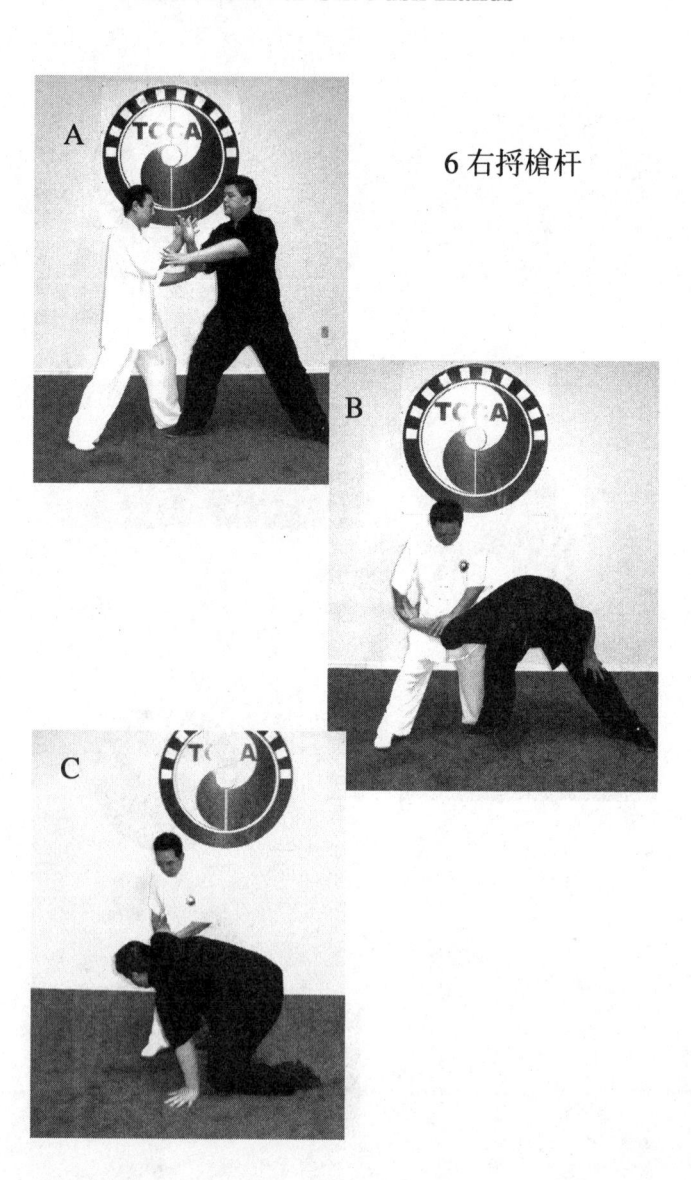

Chapter 6 Zhao Bao Tai Chi Kung Fu

Zhao Bao Tai Chi Push Hands

6 右捋槍杆

244

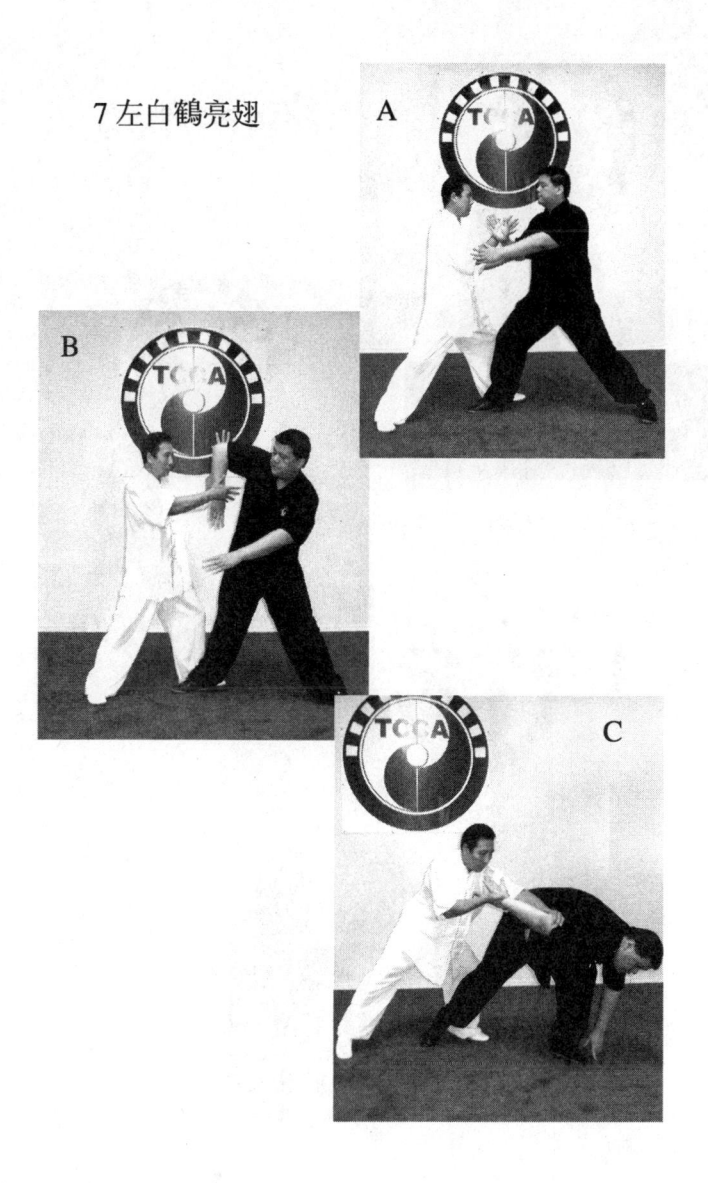

Chapter 6 Zhao Bao Tai Chi Kung Fu

Zhao Bao Tai Chi Push Hands

7 左白鶴亮翅

245

Chapter 6 Zhao Bao Tai Chi Kung Fu

Zhao Bao Tai Chi Push Hands

8 右白鶴亮翅

Zhao Bao Tai Chi Push Hands

9 肋下靠

Chapter 6 Zhao Bao Tai Chi Kung Fu

Zhao Bao Tai Chi Push Hands

10 反叠衣

2. Zhao Bao Tai Chi Qin Na (Grappling)
趙堡太極擒拿技法

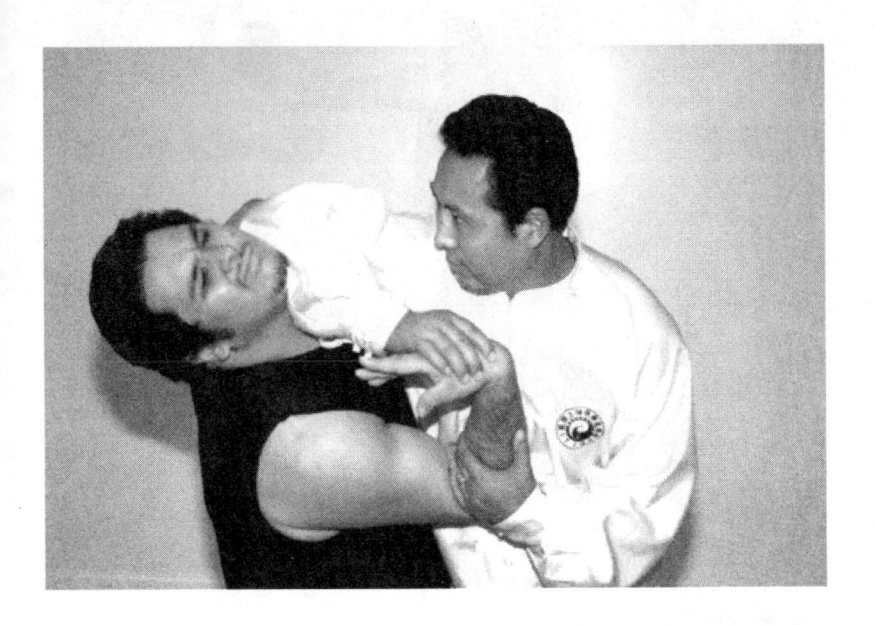

Chapter 6 Zhao Bao Tai Chi Kung Fu

Zhao Bao Tai Chi Qin Na (Grappling)

1 金絲纏腕

Chapter 6 Zhao Bao Tai Chi Kung Fu

Zhao Bao Tai Chi Qin Na (Grappling)

2 頭拿法

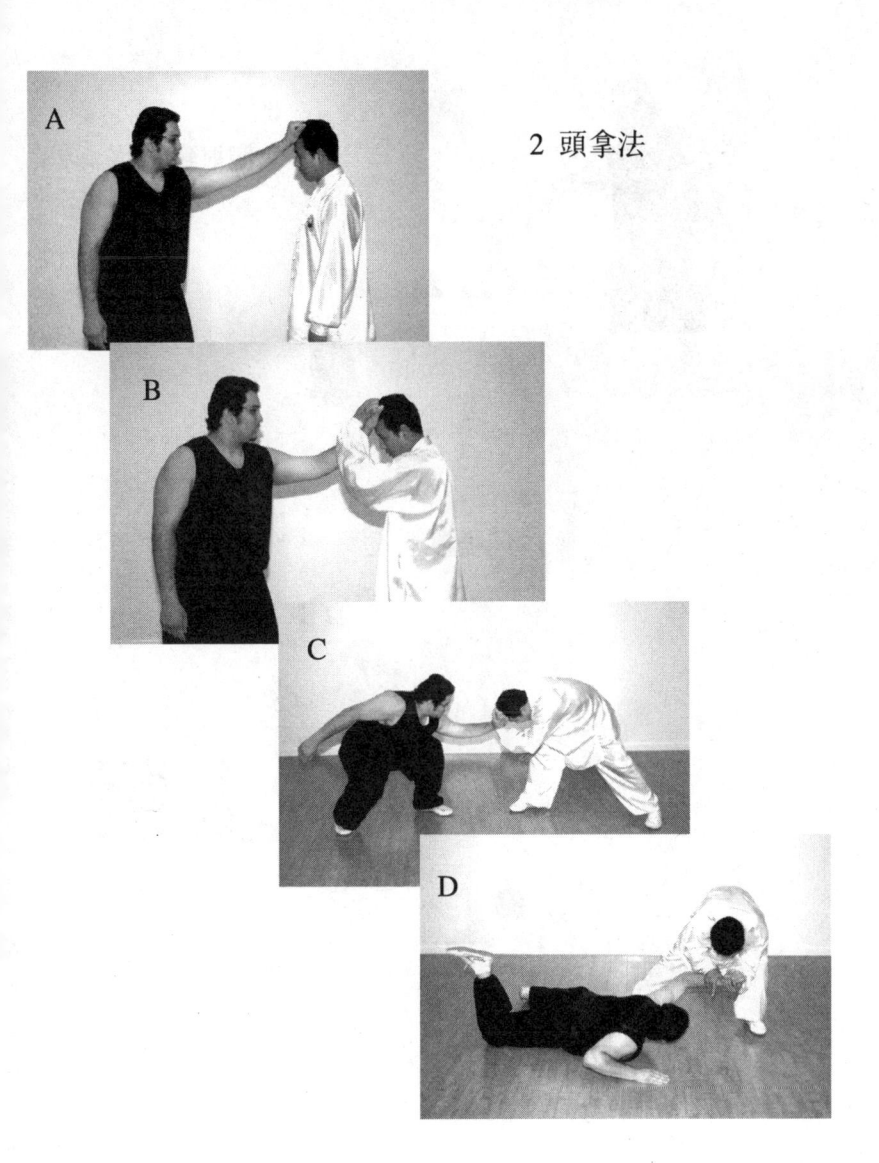

Chapter 6 Zhao Bao Tai Chi Kung Fu

Zhao Bao Tai Chi Qin Na (Grappling)

3 鐵肘鎖腕

Chapter 6 Zhao Bao Tai Chi Kung Fu

Zhao Bao Tai Chi Qin Na (Grappling)

4 鷂子搬肩

253

Chapter 6 Zhao Bao Tai Chi Kung Fu

Zhao Bao Tai Chi Qin Na (Grappling)

5 胸拿法

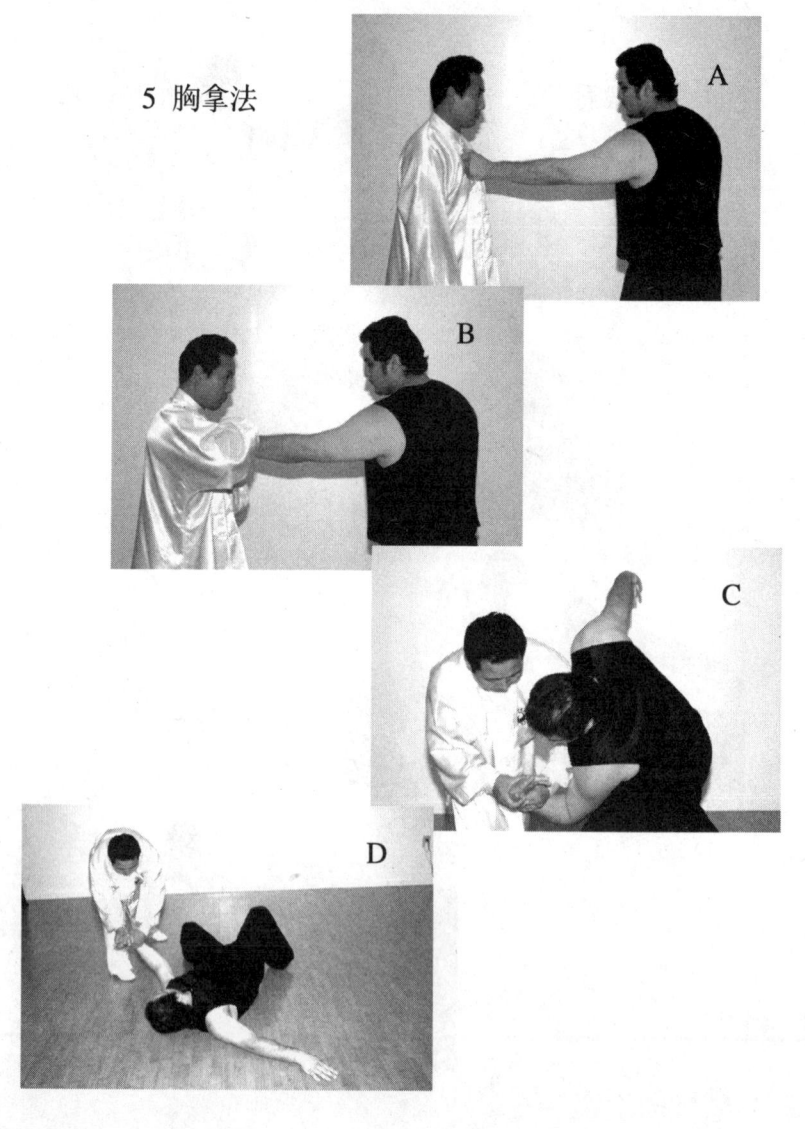

Chapter 6 Zhao Bao Tai Chi Kung Fu

Zhao Bao Tai Chi Qin Na (Grappling)

6 拜佛式

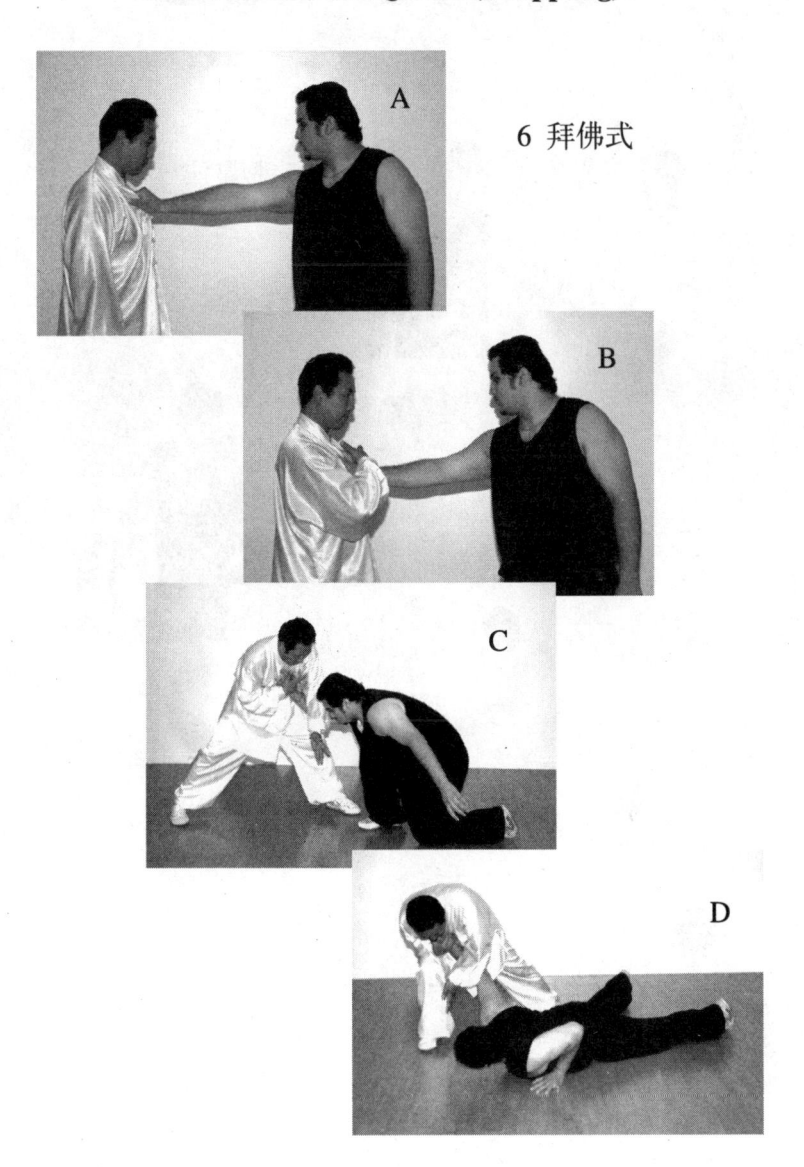

Chapter 6 Zhao Bao Tai Chi Kung Fu

Zhao Bao Tai Chi Qin Na (Grappling)

7 腕拿法

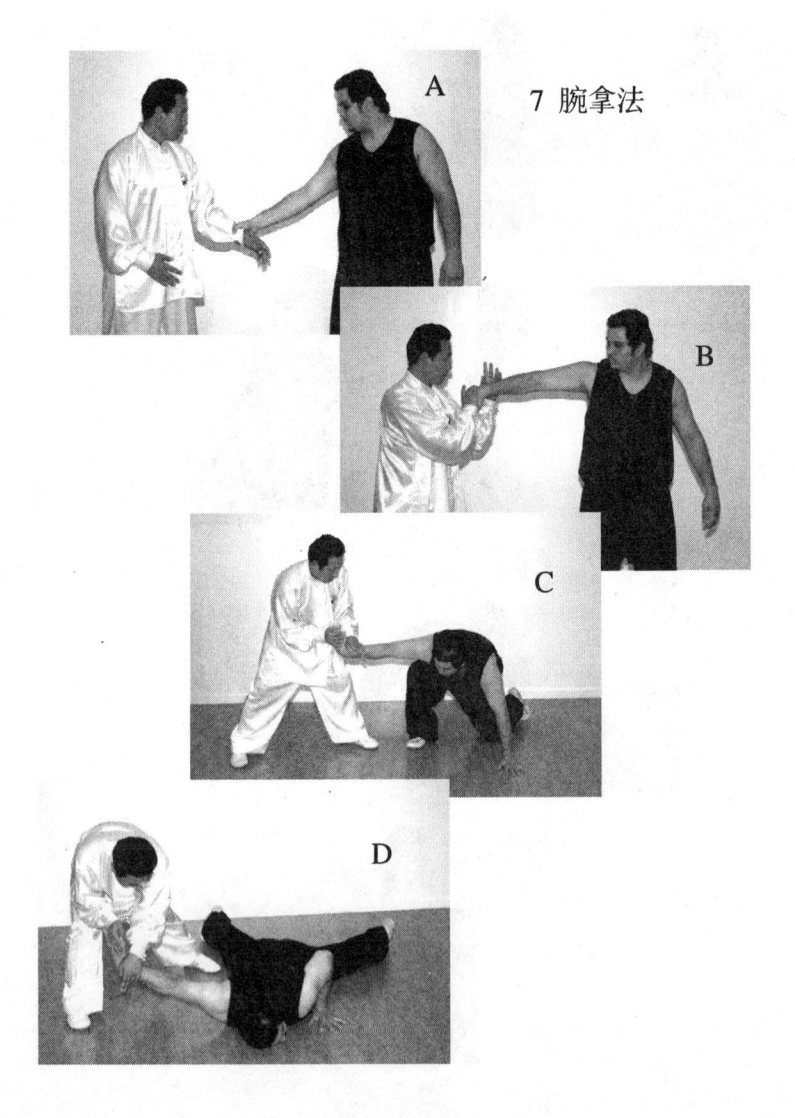

Chapter 6 Zhao Bao Tai Chi Kung Fu

Zhao Bao Tai Chi Qin Na (Grappling)

8 肘拿法

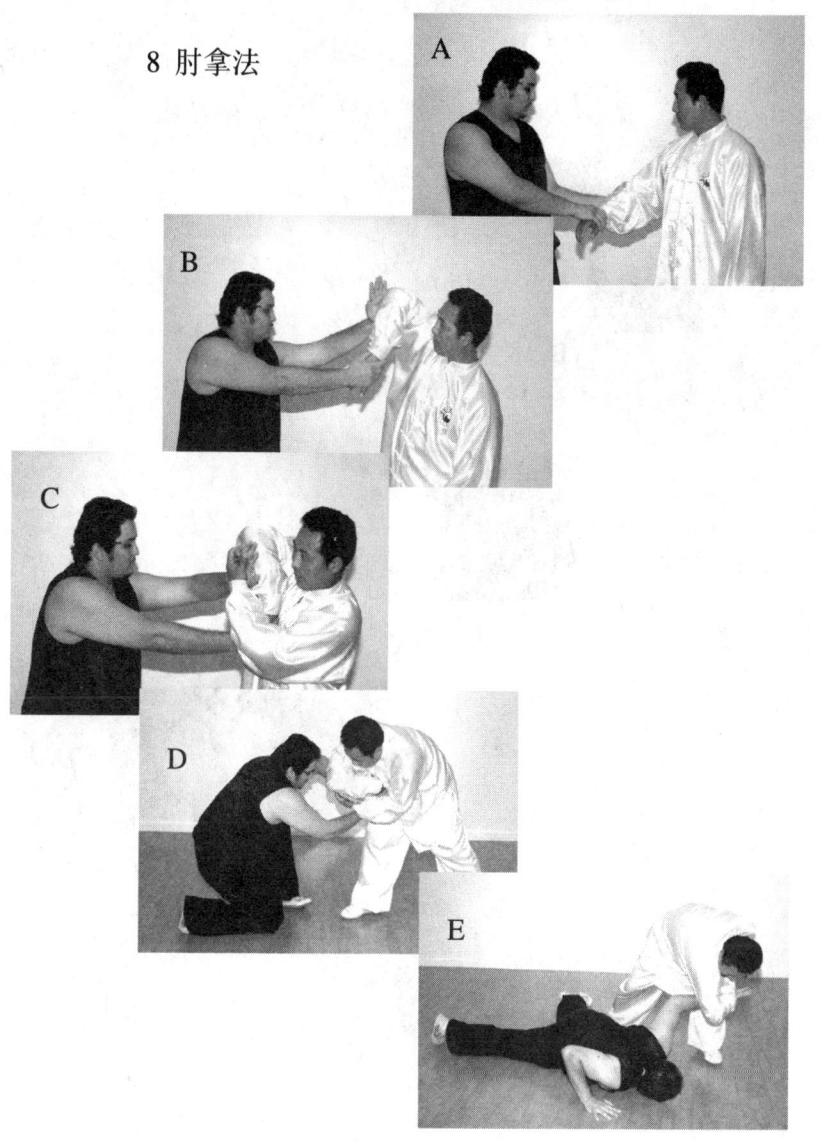

257

Chapter 6 Zhao Bao Tai Chi Kung Fu

Zhao Bao Tai Chi Qin Na (Grappling)

9 解领扣

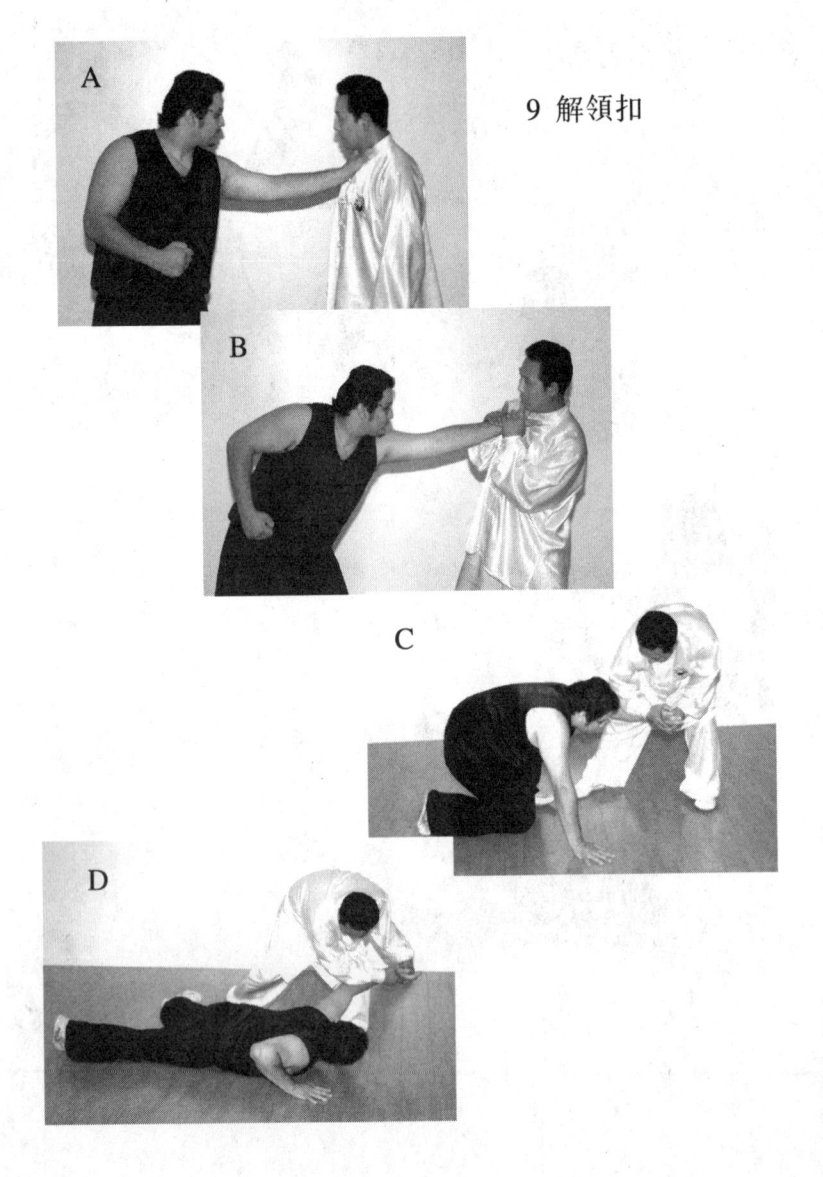

Chapter 6 Zhao Bao Tai Chi Kung Fu

Zhao Bao Tai Chi Qin Na (Grappling)

10 左捌肘

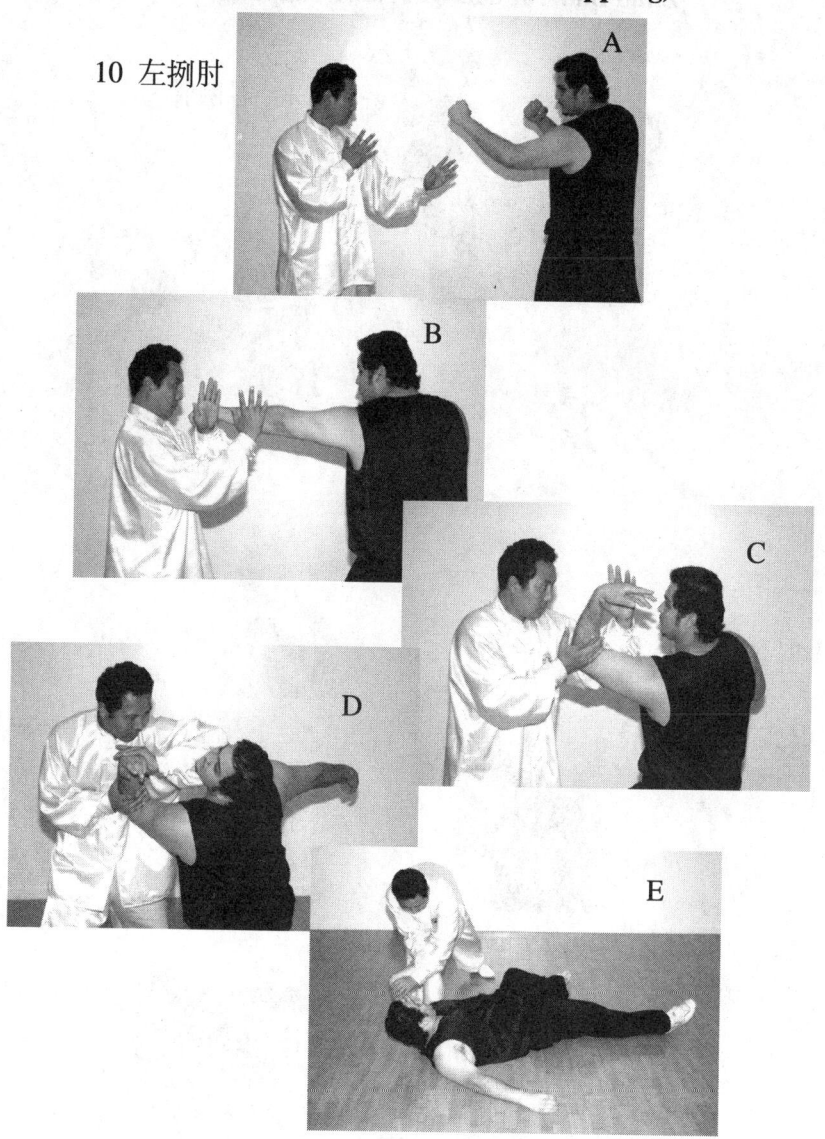

Chapter 6 Zhao Bao Tai Chi Kung Fu

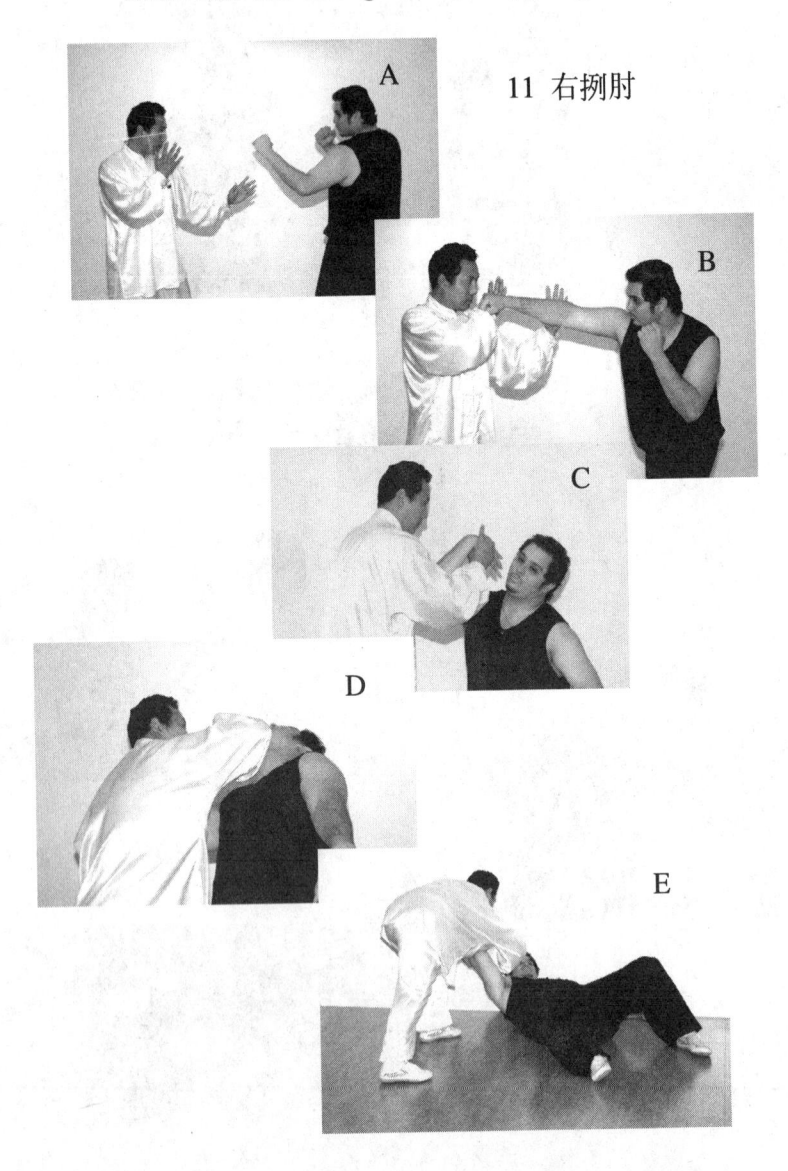

Zhao Bao Tai Chi Qin Na (Grappling)

11 右捌肘

Chapter 6 Zhao Bao Tai Chi Kung Fu

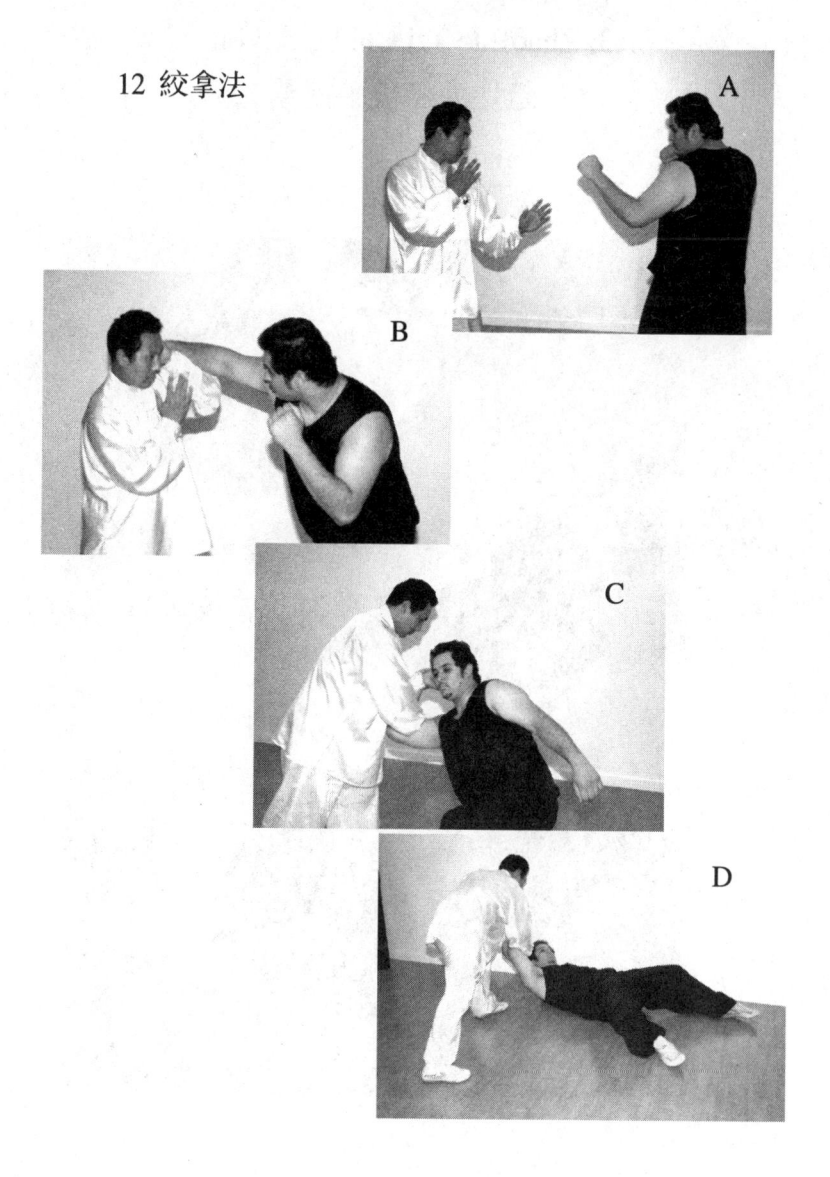

Zhao Bao Tai Chi Qin Na (Grappling)

12 絞拿法

Chapter 6 Zhao Bao Tai Chi Kung Fu

3. ZhaoBao Tai Chi San Shou
趙堡太極散手搏擊

Chapter 6 Zhao Bao Tai Chi Kung Fu

ZhaoBaoTai Chi San Shou

1

Chapter 6 Zhao Bao Tai Chi Kung Fu

ZhaoBaoTai Chi San Shou

2

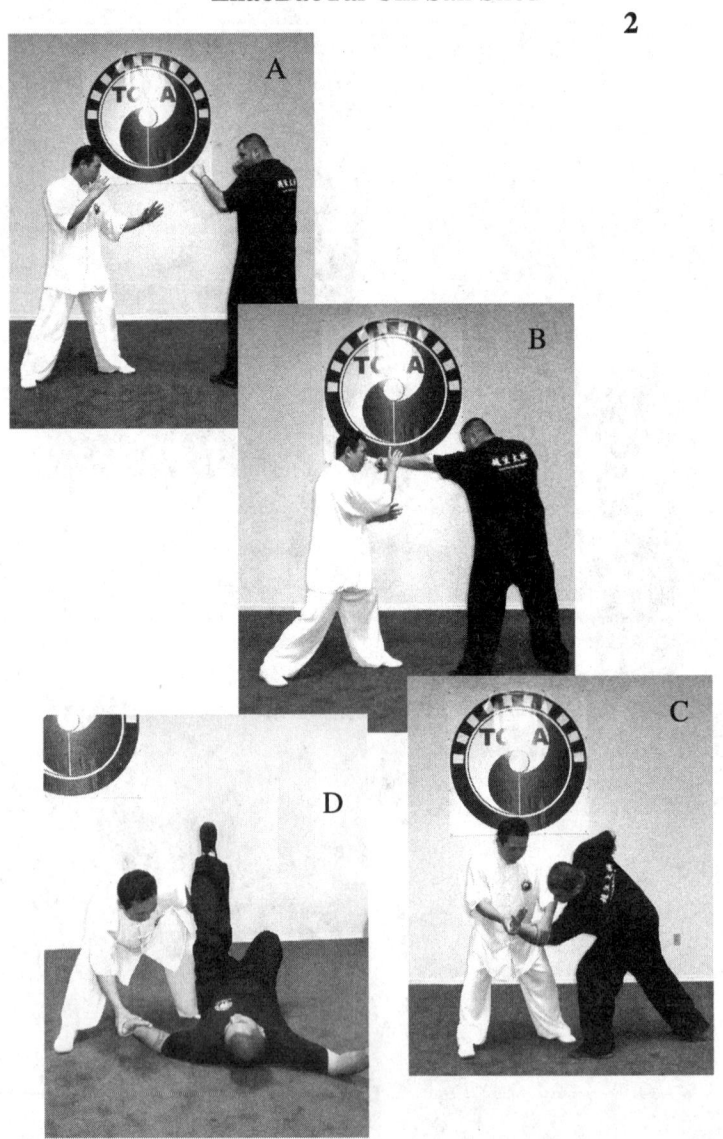

Chapter 6 Zhao Bao Tai Chi Kung Fu

ZhaoBaoTai Chi San Shou

3

265

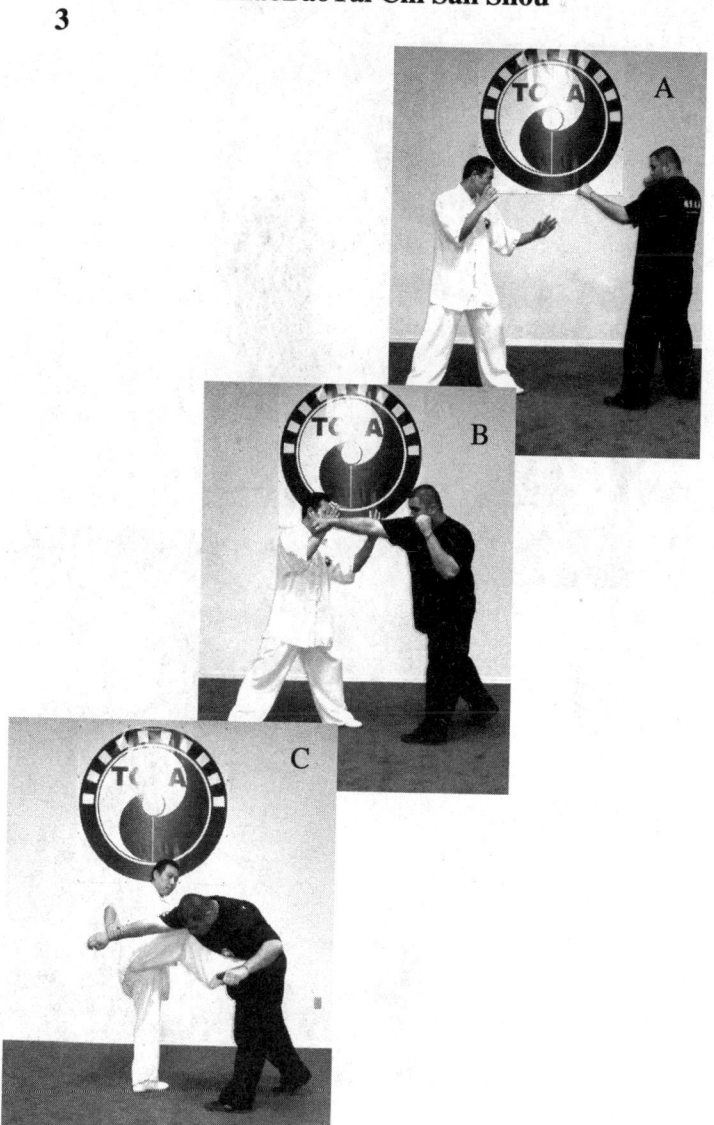

Chapter 6 Zhao Bao Tai Chi Kung Fu

ZhaoBaoTai Chi San Shou

4

A

B

Chapter 6 Zhao Bao Tai Chi Kung Fu

ZhaoBaoTai Chi San Shou

5

A

B

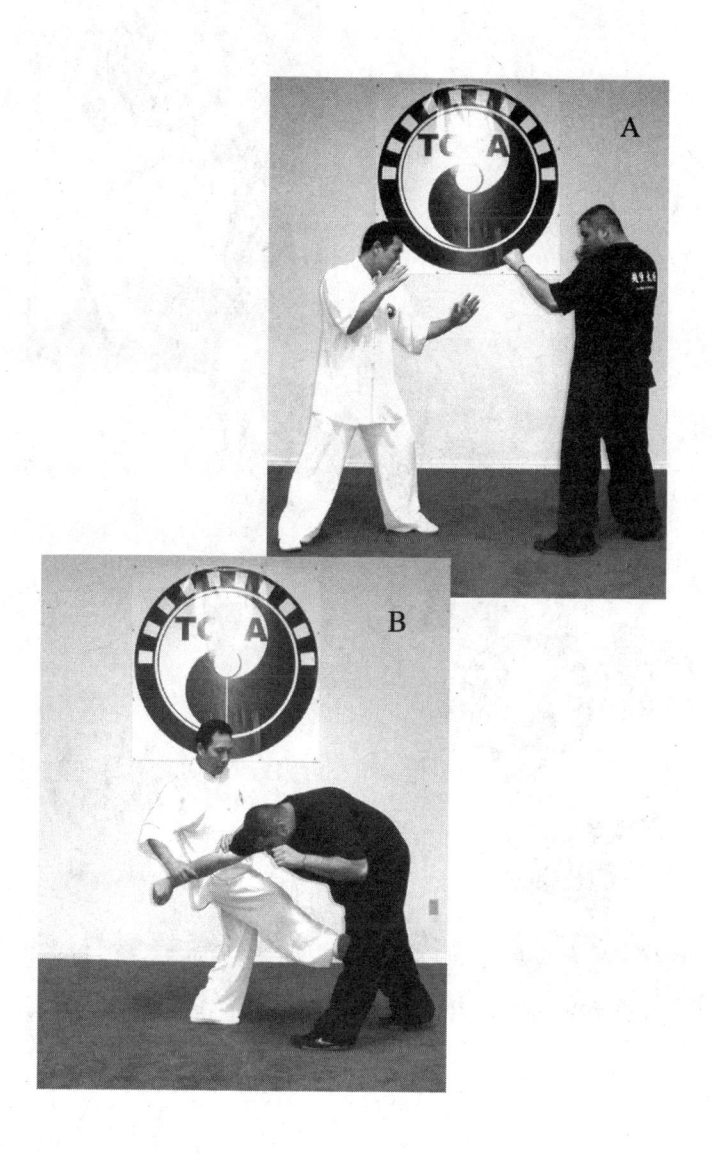

Chapter 6 Zhao Bao Tai Chi Kung Fu

ZhaoBaoTai Chi San Shou

6

Chapter 6 Zhao Bao Tai Chi Kung Fu

ZhaoBaoTai Chi San Shou

7

Chapter 6　Zhao Bao Tai Chi Kung Fu

ZhaoBaoTai Chi San Shou

8

Chapter 6 Zhao Bao Tai Chi Kung Fu

ZhaoBaoTai Chi San Shou

9

A

B

Chapter 6 Zhao Bao Tai Chi Kung Fu

ZhaoBaoTai Chi San Shou
10

Chapter 6 Zhao Bao Tai Chi Kung Fu

ZhaoBaoTai Chi San Shou

11

A

B

C

D

273

Chapter 6 Zhao Bao Tai Chi Kung Fu

ZhaoBaoTai Chi San Shou

12

A

B

C

D

Afterword

After a rigidly precise process of planning, writing, and translating, this book *Zhaobao Taichi Kongfu* is finally finished. I want to take this opportunity to thank Mr. Zongjie Yang, the managing editor of the Chinese magazine *Tai Chi*, and Mr. Shouyu Liang, the chairman of the International Wushu Sanshoudao Association, for their prefaces and kind words. While I was arranging and writing the material, several of my taichi students helped me: Yuhwa Liao Rozelle, who teaches Chinese language and culture at Stanford University, worked hard on the English translation, Shuh-hai Wong, Sophia Bo Zhou and Steven Quan to photographed, edited intensively, Wei Jim Lai and Henry Carrabello helped me to demonstrate push-hands and grappling postures for fighting, and Shiaw-Ling Lai and Ed Yu helped me by translating some articles. I thank these students for their participation and contribution.

I have loved Chinese traditional culture and martial arts since I was a child. I traveled widely and looked for great masters to learn taichi and kungfu of many different schools. I especially loved the techniques of modern wushu san shou. In 1980 I was fortunate to become the disciple of Yunhua Song, who was a world-renowned grandmaster in martial arts and the 11th generation master of Zhaobao Taichi Kungfu. I studied Zhaobao Taichi Kungfu and many fighting techniques with him. At first, I was young and arrogant, and proud to be able to fight with everybody. Following my respected teacher everywhere inside and outside of China to disseminate Zhaobao Taichi Kungfu, I met many people and learned many things. I became more mature. With Mr. Song's teaching, I practiced hard every day, and thought about strategy day and night.

Afterword

I gradually came to understand the profundity of Zhaobao Taichi Kungfu. The profound world of taichi is like the deep ocean that makes you wonder. There are millions of people searching for taichi kungfu, but there are only a few who truly get it in each generation. It takes a long time to reach the goal. Every taichi practitioner has a lot of questions in the beginning and meets all kinds of problems in the course of practice. I hope these taichi lovers will find that this book *Zhaobao Taichi Kungfu* helps them. And I hope it will benefit their health as well.

I dedicate this book to the memory of my beloved teacher Mr. Song, who is no longer with us. For my whole life I will follow his footsteps and keep alive his will to disseminate Zhaobao Taichi Kungfu.

Wayne Peng
September, 2008 at San Francisco

編后語

《趙堡太極拳》一書經過緊鑼密鼓的籌劃和撰寫以及英文翻譯，目前已經脫稿；在此要特別感謝中國太極雜志社社長兼總編楊宗杰先生、國際武術散手道聯盟主席梁守渝先生在百忙之中分別為本書作序；在整理書稿期間，得力于我的太極學生、任職斯坦佛大學漢語教授的廖玉華女士為本書的英文翻譯做出了辛勤的工作，以及王樹海、周波和關信義在攝影及編輯整理等方面做出了大量的工作，賴偉堅和 Henry Carrabello 在本書推手擒拿技擊欄目作相關動作姿勢示範，還有賴孝凌和俞亮之前在"概論"、"源流"、"簡介"等篇做出了相應的翻譯工作；對眾弟子的熱心參與和付出，我在此一并表示感謝。

　　余自幼酷愛傳統文化及武術，年少好勇，于民間廣尋名師遍習各門各派之拳架功法，尤其對功夫散打技擊之強對抗嗜之特甚；有幸于八零年拜列世界著名武術家、當世一代太極巨擘、中國趙堡太極拳第十一代宗師宋蘊華先生門下，習練趙堡太極拳傳統功夫各項技藝；初因年幼氣盛，對太極功夫之認知甚淺，終日以現代搏擊之雄為能事，后追隨恩師南北奔波，四處傳播趙堡太極拳藝，足跡遍踏海內外，其間廣見博聞，日漸成熟，在恩師言傳身教之下，終日習練，徹夜思悟，苦心追求，不敢半點懈怠，方有點滴感悟，漸漸探知趙堡太極之堂奧。然論及太極境界之玄妙莫測，太極內涵之浩如烟海，不勝感慨之至；世人追求太極功夫者數以千萬計，然成手者代不過數人；誠然千里之行始于足下，九層之臺起于累土，每個太極功夫的追求者在其習練的過程中都會遇到各種各樣的問題；惟願《趙堡太極拳》一書能夠為廣大的太極拳愛好者提供幫助，也希望更多追求身體健康的人們能從中受益。

　　在此亦借此書追思先師在天之英靈，定當追隨恩師之志，終生廣傳趙堡太極拳藝，使之發揚光大。

　　　　　　　　　　　　　　　　彭文
　　　　　　　　　　　二零零八年九月　于舊金山

To the Readers

The purpose of this book *Zhaobao Taichi Kongfu* from Mr. Wayne Peng, the chairman of the USA Tai Chi Culture Association and a 12th generation successor of Zhaobao Taichi Kungfu, is to help all taichi lovers. If you have any problems in understanding this book or any questions about practicing Zhaobao Taichi, you may email him. If you happen to be in the San Francisco Bay Area and wish to take lessons from him, you may email him to make arrangements. He answers each email.

The USA Tai Chi Culture Association will continue to publish books in both Chinese and English for you. Future books in the series will be *Zhaobao Taichi Push-Hands, Zhaobao Taichi Sword, Zhaobao Taichi Stick,* and *Zhaobao Taichi Grappling Techniques,* among others. The series will give taichi lovers a complete picture of traditional Zhaobao Taichi Kungfu and help them enjoy it.

USA Tai Chi Culture Association
Telephone: 1- 408-262-3867   1- 510-739-1832
Mailing address: P.O.Box 361551, Milpitas, CA95036
E-mail: tcca@usataichikungfu.com
Website: www.usataichikungfu.com
Address: 1344 Ridder Park Drive, San Jose
                CA 95131, USA

To the Readers

致讀者

　　美國太極文化協會會長、中國趙堡太極拳第十二代傳人彭文先生出版的這本《趙堡太極拳》一書，致力于為廣大的太極拳愛好者提供幫助，讀者在閱覽、學練時如有任何疑難問題，可來函致電垂詢，若需面授研修，敬請提前預約聯系，來函必復，來電必答。

　　美國太極文化協會今后將會陸續出版面世中、英文對照版：《趙堡太極推手》、《趙堡太極劍》、《趙堡太極棍》、《趙堡太極實用擒拿格斗》等系列叢書，全面揭示趙堡太極傳統功夫各項技藝。以饗讀者。

美國太極文化協會

電話：　　　1-408-262-3867
　　　　　　1-510-739-1832
郵政信箱：　P.O.Box 361551
　　　　　　Milpitas, CA95036, USA
電子信箱：　tcca@usataichikungfu.com
網址：　　　www.usataichikungfu.com
地址：　　　1344 Ridder Park Drive, San Jose
　　　　　　CA 95131, USA